What Makes Me Feel Safe

Women's Stories about Peace, War, Human Rights

What Makes Me Feel Safe

Women's Stories about Peace, War, Human Rights

Collected and edited by Annemarie Sancar and Heidi Meinzolt

Published by the Working Group on Women and Gender Realities in the OSCE Area in the Civic Solidarity Platform, on the occasion of the 2024 OSCE Malta Conference

https://civicsolidarity.org/member/1451/working-group-women-and-gender-realities-osce-region/

CIVIC SOLIDARITY

Thanks to the donor

Government Offices of Sweden
Ministry for Foreign Affairs

Layout: Peter Pich

München 2024

FSC
www.fsc.org
MIX
Papier aus verantwortungsvollen Quellen
Paper from responsible sources
FSC® C105338

Bibliografische Information der Deutschen Nationalbibliothek

Die Deutsche Nationalbibliothek verzeichnet diese Publikation in der Deutschen Nationalbibliografie; detaillierte bibliografische Daten sind im Internet über http://dnb.d-nb.de abrufbar.

Verlag: BoD · Books on Demand GmbH, In de Tarpen 42, 22848 Norderstedt
Druck: Libri Plureos GmbH, Friedensallee 273, 22763 Hamburg

ISBN: 978-3-7597-8465-0

Content

What Makes Me Feel Safe – Preface

A collection of stories about security and insecurity – from women's diverse realities, compiled by Heidi Meinzolt und Annemarie Sancar, 2024.

> *„Stories and storytelling cover a vital role in the peacebuilding process and the transformation of peoples' lives, especially post-conflict … storytelling is the process of imagination for individuals and communities,. value local knowledge in creating cross-cultural contexts and amplifying voices muted by dominant hegemony … Without imagination, we cannot reach a significant meaning of cultures, relationships, systems, and we cannot analyse how conflicts are created … As a feminist approach, care ethics are to be claimed as a critical asset to the storytelling process … Stories are a way of presenting our care about our past, present, and future … people can live through stories and change through stories … Storytelling is a process where we say that each life matters and all lives matter …"*
>
> *(Excerpt from a master thesis of Yara El Harake „Stories Matter: A process of care for storytelling in peacebuilding", Barcelona 2021)*

Security is a concept that has been increasingly dominated by the militaristic narrative in recent years. Today, the language of security is primarily used in the context of armament, defence, 'civil protection' ... This always takes place in a dual system of thought of friend and foe, good and evil, victim and perpetrator. These poles are supposedly irreconcilably opposed to each other - without any spaces or positions in between. From a feminist perspective, this duality interests us in various ways: it symbolises a narrowing of the concept of security and triggers feelings of insecurity in many people. Insecurity, in turn, can be instrumentalised to get people to vote for military protection, i.e. protection through weapons. This makes it easier to divert money flows on the basis of the narrative distortion of what security can mean.

We women are interested in the concept of security because we know from our experience and from working with women and women's organisations that security has many facets in everyday life: It is about health, sexual and reproductive rights, education, access to resources and politically relevant decisions, social security and care as well as a life in dignity without violence. This complex understanding of security must be constantly and critically scrutinised. In practice, this means training in non-violent conflict resolution, giving early warning of possible conflict escalation and showing ways to achieve reconciliation. The increasing shift of resources away from welfare state institutions towards surveillance technologies and institutions that use violence, such as the military or police, stand in the way of this endeavour. Feminist peace politics and feminist tracing of paths to peace should therefore shed light on the diverse meanings and different understandings of security in both private and collective public contexts. This collection of stories about security and what it has to do with peace is as diverse and multi-layered as the lives and life plans of the women we asked and who wanted to write something.

The method of storytelling seems to us to be suitable for giving space to the images of security, experiences of security and feelings of security of a wide variety of women (in the OSCE area and in the Middle East). The stories can also be linked to symbolic and artistic forms of expression. They oscillate between the poles of insecurity and security, and provide food for thought as to what one's own contribution could be to expanding the paths to peace. In the moment of writing, the authors give expression to despair, hope and the longing for solidarity. The aim is to recognise, name and overcome inner resistance.

This is not least due to the fact that social constraints put women under pressure to bow to the glorification myth of the 'brave fighters for the nation', the 'patriots', to admire militarised masculinity and to internalise it as the only positive gender dispositive. This makes it difficult to criticise the patriarchal social order that is thus reinforced. Particularly in times of war, the pressure to conform and the discrediting of pacifist attitudes grows to the point of public denigration and criminalisation.

Mainstream media are interested in disaster stories. This closes windows for critical perspectives. There is a need for strong dissenting voices that lead back from geostrategic power politics to the human dimension of war and violence and develop a preventive agenda that is also reflected financially in the areas of life relevant to the welfare state.

Safe spaces and an atmosphere where women can tell their stories for themselves and for others are needed more than ever. This is also the prerequisite for readers to think about a peaceful life at all and to organise their everyday living conditions in such a way that caring for themselves and others makes a dignified life possible.

On the occasion of the handover of the OSCE chairmanship from Malta to Finland, december 2024, we will present these stories to discuss ways to peace and safety to bring aspects of feminist civil society also into the institutions.

We thank all women authors for their precious contributions.

Heidi Meinzolt and Annemarie Sancar, November 2024

Was macht mich sicher – Vorwort

Eine Sammlung von Geschichten über Sicherheit und Unsicherheit aus feministischen Perspektiven, zusammengestellt von Heidi Meinzolt und Annemarie Sancar, 2024

Sicherheit ist ein Begriff, der in den letzten Jahren zunehmend vom militaristischen Umfeld von Aufrüstung, Verteidigung, 'Bevölkerungsschutz' … Dies geschieht immer in einem dualen Denksystem von Freund und Feind, Gut und Böse, Opfer und Täter. Diese Pole stehen sich angeblich unversöhnlich einander gegenüber – ohne Zwischenräume oder -positionen. Aus der feministischen Perspektive interessiert uns diese Dualität in verschiedener Hinsicht: Sie symbolisiert eine Einengung des Begriffs der Sicherheit und löst bei vielen Menschen Unsicherheitsgefühle aus. Unsicherheit wiederum lässt sich instrumentalisieren, um die Menschen dazu zu bringen, für militärischen Schutz, d.h. Schutz durch Waffen zu votieren. So fällt es leichter, Geldströme umzuleiten, und zwar auf der Basis der narrativen Verdrehung dessen, was Sicherheit bedeuten kann.

Uns Frauen interessiert der Begriff Sicherheit, weil wir aufgrund unserer Erfahrung und aus der Zusammenarbeit mit Frauen und Frauenorganisationen wissen, dass Sicherheit im Alltag viele Facetten hat: Es geht um Gesundheit, sexuelle und reproduktive Rechte, Bildung, Zugang zu Ressourcen und politisch relevanten Entscheidungen, soziale Sicherheit und Sorge sowie ein Leben in Würde ohne Gewalt. Dieses komplexe Verständnis von Sicherheit muss immer wieder neu und kritisch durchleuchtet werden. In der Praxis bedeutet dies, gewaltfreie Konfliktlösung zu trainieren, früh vor möglicher Konflikteskalation zu warnen und Wege zu Versöhnung aufzuzeigen. Die zunehmende Verschiebung von Ressourcen weg von wohlfahrtsstaatlichen Einrichtungen hin zu Überwachungstechnologien und Gewalt ausübenden Institutionen wie Militär oder Polizei stehen diesem Anliegen im Wege.

Feministische Friedenspolitik, feministische Spurensetzung auf Wegen zum Frieden sollen deshalb die mannigfaltigen Bedeutungen, die unterschiedlichen Verständnisse von Sicherheit im privaten wie im kollektiven öffentlichen Rahmen beleuchten. Diese Sammlung von Geschichten zu Sicherheit und was es dabei mit Frieden auf sich hat, ist so vielfältig und vielschichtig wie die Lebenswege und Lebensentwürfe der Frauen, die wir gefragt haben und die gerne etwas schreiben wollten.

Die Methode des Geschichtenerzählens scheint uns geeignet den Sicherheitsbildern, Sicherheitserfahrungen und Sicherheitsgefühlen von verschiedensten Frauen (im OSZE Raum und im Nahen Osten) Raum zu geben. Die Geschichten können auch mit symbolischer und künstlerischer Ausdrucksform verbunden sein. Sie pendeln zwischen den Polen von Unsicherheiten und Sicherheiten, und liefern Denkanstöße, was der eigene Beitrag zum Ausbau der Wege hin zu Frieden sein könnte. Die Autorinnen geben im Moment des Schreibens der Verzweiflung, der Hoffnung und der Sehnsucht nach Solidarität Ausdruck. Dabei gilt es, innere Widerstände zu erkennen, zu benennen und zu überwinden.

Das liegt nicht zuletzt daran, dass die gesellschaftlichen Zwänge Frauen unter Druck setzen, sich dem Verherrlichungsmythos der „mutigen Kämpfer für die Nation", der „Patriot*innen", zu beugen, die militarisierte Männlichkeit zu bewundern und als einziges positives Geschlechterdispositiv zu verinnerlichen. So wird Kritik an der damit bekräftigten patriarchalen Gesellschaftsordnung erschwert. Gerade in Kriegszeiten wächst der Anpassungsdruck und die Diskreditierung pazifistischer Einstellung bis hin zur öffentlichen Verunglimpfung und Kriminalisierung.

Mainstreammedien interessieren sich für Katastrophenstorys. Damit schliessen sich Fenster für kritische Sichtweisen. Es braucht starke Gegenstimmen, die von geostrategischer Machtpolitik wieder auf die menschliche Dimension von Krieg und Gewalt zurückführen und daraus eine präventive Agenda entwickeln, die sich auch finanziell in den sozialstaatlich relevanten Lebensbereichen niederschlägt.

Sichere Räume und eine Stimmung, wo Frauen ihre Geschichte für sich und für andere erzählen können, sind mehr denn je notwendig. Auch für Leser*innen ist dies die Voraussetzung, ein friedliches Leben überhaupt zu denken und die alltagsbedingten Lebensumstände so einzurichten, dass die Sorge für sich und andere ein würdiges Leben ermöglicht.

Anlässlich der Übergabe des OSZE Vorsitzes von Malta an Finnland Dezember 2024 werden wir diese Geschichten vorstellen, um Wege zu Frieden und Sicherheit zu diskutieren und Aspekte der feministischen Zivilgesellschaft auch in die Institutionen einzubringen.

Wir danken allen Autorinnen für ihre wertvollen Beiträge.

Heidi Meinzolt und Annemarie Sancar, November 2024

What Makes Me Feel Safe

Ruth Gaby Vermot, *former member of the Swiss Parliament and the European Council, Co-founder of 1000 Women for the Peace Nobel Price 2005 and president of the Organisation PeaceWomen Across the Globe PWAG.*

I grew up with four siblings, my parents were day labourers, my father was quite argumentative, the flat was tiny, the money was used up by the end of the month, I had few friends because 'you don't play with dirty children', I was a good pupil, left-handed and punished for not being right-handed. I got into fights with the boys, was loud and certainly unsympathetic. There was only one book at home, 'Viamala' by John Knittel. But the main character fell into the Viamala gorge – not a heroic role model either! I was supposed to do an office apprenticeship and my wish to study and do my A-levels was waved away. Girls and young people like me weren't part of the elite. Our parents loved us – sure – but there wasn't much time ... it was the fault of lousy wages and the long working hours into the night!

Security? The banal security, i.e. a kind of reliable, confidence-building, basic emotional provision, such as a good flat, being healthy, good food – not just a sausage for seven, enough money in a bank account, clean or even new clothes, friends, recognition, appreciation, attention, understanding teachers, a caring family or support in difficult times – all this was available in minimal quantities. I hardly experienced any reliable and strengthening security, I had to pick it up again and again in fragments – that's my picture in retrospect. And to be honest, I still feel that way today, because I never experience security as stable. Security is always fragile and breakable!

As a member of the National Council and the Council of Europe, I dealt with issues such as migration, asylum, trafficking in women, children and organs, violence against women and violence against children. Opponents of my political positions penalised me with mounds of ghouls outside my door, death threats and other disparaging acts. Even though I fought against it, the massive violence from unknown opponents made me feel insecure. Only long-term police protection helped me to put the pieces of my security back together again.

Today's world with its many wars, the destruction caused by ever more dangerous weapons systems, the permanent armament, armed security, the climate problem and the millions of refugees unsettles me deeply. This drunkenness of war and the malicious killing, the patriarchy set in stone and the intransigence of all the warmongers like the Bidens, the Putins and Nethanjahus, the Kim-Jong-uns and the Bassars or Xi Jinpings, who only know one answer to conflicts and their wounded masculinity: wars and destruction. The certainty that we will live in a peaceful world tomorrow, that my grandchildren and my daughters will have a future, that relationships will not be torn apart and that human rights will remain alive, is becoming more questionable every day. It takes my breath away, my security crumbles. And again I pick up the pieces and try to reassemble them into a secure safety.

Peace, with its fragility and completely different dynamic, makes me feel secure. The hope for peace, which careful women and people often work on for years, makes me feel safe. Peace, justice, solidarity and mindfulness are perhaps the brackets that provide living security.

Was macht mich sicher

Ruth-Gaby Vermot, *Schweiz, ehem. Mitglied des Schweizer Parlaments und des Europarates, Mitbegründerin von „1000 Frauen für den Friedensnobelpreis 2005" und Präsidentin der Nachfolgeorganisation PeaceWomen Across the Globe PWAG.*

Aufgewachsen bin ich mit vier Geschwistern, die Eltern waren Taglöhner, der Vater ziemlich streitsüchtig, die Wohnung winzig, das Geld gegen Monatsende aufgebraucht, wenig Freund:innen, denn „mit Schmuddelkindern spielt man nicht", gute Schülerin, Linkshänderin die man zur Rechtshänderin bestrafte. Ich prügelte mich mit den Jungs, war laut und sicher auch unsympathisch. Zuhause gab es ein einziges Buch, „Viamala" von John Knittel. Aber der Hauptdarsteller fiel in die Viamala-Schlucht – also auch kein heldenhaftes Vorbild! Ich sollte eine Bürolehre machen, meinen Wunsch, zu studieren, die Matura zu machen, wedelte man weg. Mädchen und Jugendliche wie ich gehörten nicht zur Elite. Die Eltern liebten uns – sicher – aber die Zeit dafür war knapp … schuld waren die miesen Taglöhne und die langen Arbeitszeiten bis in die Nacht!

Sicherheit? Die banale Sicherheit, also eine Art verlässliche, vertrauensbildende, emotionale Grundversorgung, wie eine gute Wohnung, gesund sein, gutes Essen - also nicht nur eine Wurst für sieben, genügend Geld auf einem Bankkonto, saubere oder gar neue Kleidung, Freund:innen, Anerkennung, Wertschätzung, Aufmerksamkeit, verständnisvolle Lehrpersonen, eine sorgsame Familie oder Unterstützung in schwierigeren Zeiten – all dies gab es in Minimengen. Ich erlebte wohl kaum verlässliche und stärkende Sicherheit, die musste ich immer wieder in Bruchstücken aufsammeln – so mein Bild im Rückblick. Und um ehrlich zu sein, so geht es mir noch heute, denn ich erlebe Sicherheit nie als stabil. Sicherheit ist immer fragil und zerbrechlich!

Als National- und Europarätin befasste ich mich unter anderem mit Migration, Asyl, Frauen-, Kinder- und Organhandel, Gewalt gegen Frauen, Gewalt gegen Kinder. Gegner:innen meiner politischen Positionen bestraften mich mit Ghüderbergen vor meiner Tür, Morddrohungen und sonst verunglimpfenden Handlungen. Auch wenn ich dagegen ankämpfte, verunsicherte mich die massive Gewalt unbekannter Widersacher:innen. Erst polizeilicher Langzeitschutz half, die Bruchstücke meiner Sicherheit wieder zusammen zu setzen.

Die heutige Welt mit den vielen Kriegen, den Zerstörungen durch immer gefährlichere Waffensysteme, der permanenten Aufrüstung, der bewaffneten Sicherheit, der Klimaproblematik und den Millionen Flüchtlingen verunsichert mich zu tiefst. Diese Kriegstrunkenheit und das böswillige Töten, das beinhart betonierte Patriarchat und die Uneinsichtigkeit all der Kriegstreiber wie die Bidens, die Putins und Nethanjahus, die Kim-Jong-uns und die Bassars oder Xi Jinpings, die nur eine Antwort auf Konflikte und ihre verletzte Männlichkeit kennen: Kriege und Zerstörung. Die Sicherheit, dass wir morgen in einer friedlichen Welt leben, dass meine Enkel, meine Töchter eine Zukunft haben, Beziehungen nicht zerreissen und die Menschenrechte lebendig bleiben, wird täglich fraglicher. Das nimmt mir den Atem, meine Sicherheit zerbröckelt. Und wieder sammle ich die Bruchstücke auf und versuche, sie zu einer sicheren Sicherheit zusammenzubauen.

Sicher macht mich Frieden mit seiner Fragilität und ganz anderen Dynamik. Sicher macht mich die Hoffnung auf Frieden, an dem sorgsame Frauen, Menschen oft jahrelang arbeiten. Frieden, Gerechtigkeit, Solidarität und Achtsamkeit sind vielleicht die Klammer, welche lebendige Sicherheit gewährt.

(In-) Certainties

***Annemarie Sancar**, Bern, Dr.phil, socialanthropologist, expert in feminist peace-building, gender justice in politics, member of WILPF CH and WIDE CH, lecturer in international cooperation and development, economic literacy and care economy.*

You are standing outside on the street and the earth is shaking. You want to hold on to the pillar, it moves, dizziness takes hold of you, everything inside and around you trembles ... great, profound insecurity and you are powerless ... Then a great fear grasps you, you lose all control, a feeling of the greatest insecurity is grabbing you.

You lose your dearest friends, they are arrested, they are banished, and you see their pictures in the newspaper, marked by torture, their faces almost unrecognisable, you are gripped by great fear, am I still safe? When will it hit me? Can I know that? How can I protect myself? Am I simply powerless, at the mercy of the powerful, at the mercy of the military audacity of men (in this case in Chile in 1985)? My every movement, every thought, everything in me is characterised by great uncertainty.

Aircraft noise, smoke, shattering windows, tear gas, screaming ... that's how you experience the first Initifada in the West Bank. The worst, most threatening thing is the military helicopters circling above you. No roof offers any more protection, a feeling of being at the mercy of others, only my friends in the room can be relied on, but it's written all over everyone's face. We feel insecure, threatened... let's hold on together, let's stick together, let's offer a wall of trust ... at least this gives us a little security.

So no peace in sight? For this we all need stability, familiarity, security, a social environment, only then will doors and windows to peace open ... but it is us, who have to find the paths, and this can only be achieved together, starting from a shared attitude, a common everyday reality, a solid basis of trust, a common project for peace.

Security ... a basic feeling, the basis for peace. For this I need certainties for my everyday life, a solid ground for strength and energy, supporting walls for my hands, clear points of orientation. We need shared memories as a starting point for the paths to a peaceful society; to have (perceived) sovereignty over our own actions, over the immediate everyday conditions, a language that creates trust ... so that I, so that we can clear away the stones together, can take the next steps.

Friends are there, they are close, and they give each other security. It is the familiar, the knowledge of not being alone, the knowledge that tomorrow there will be no alarm, that tomorrow we will be able to breathe clean air, eat good food, have clean water, work. We need the security of knowing that we can fulfil our everyday needs, meet, exchange ideas and take action. It is the security of not being alone ... that gives the necessary calm, security, stability, trust, as an indispensable basis for peace.

(Un-) Sicherheiten

***Annemarie Sancar**, Bern.*

Du stehst draussen auf der Strasse, und die Erde bebt. Du willst dich am Pfeiler halten, dieser bewegt sich, Schwindel ergreift sich, alles in dir und um dich zittert … grosse, tiefgehende Verunsicherung und du bist machtlos … Dann erfasst dich grosse Angst, du verlierst jeglichen Halt, dich ergreift ein Gefühl grösster Unsicherheit.

Du verlierst deine liebsten Freundinnen, sie werden verhaftet, sie werden verbannt, du siehst ihre Bilder in der Zeitung, gezeichnet von Folter, fast nicht erkennbar ihre Gesichter, dich ergreift grosse Angst, bin ich noch sicher? Wann trifft es mich? Kann ich das wissen? Wie kann ich mich schützen? Bin ich einfach machtlos, den Mächtigen ausgeliefert, der militärischen Dreistigkeit der Männer (in diesem Fall in Chile 1985)? Jede meiner Bewegungen, jeder Gedanke, alles in mir ist geprägt von grosser Unsicherheit.

Fluglärm, Rauch, berstende Scheiben, beissendes Tränengas, Geschrei … so erlebst du die erste Initifada im Westjordanland. Das schlimmste, bedrohlichste sind die Militärhelikopter, die über dir kreisen … kein Dach bietet mehr Schutz, ein Gefühl des Ausgeliefertseins, nur auf meine Freunde im Raum ist Verlass, doch allen ist ins Gesicht geschrieben ... wir fühlen uns unsicher, bedroht ... halten wir uns gemeinsam fest, halten wir zusammen, bieten wir eine Mauer des Vertrauens ... wenigstens gibt uns dies ein bisschen Sicherheit.

Kein Friede in Sicht also? Dafür brauchen wir alle Stabilität, Vertrautheiten, Sicherheit, ein soziales Umfeld, erst dann öffnen sich Türen und Fenster zum Frieden... Die Wege aber müssen wir finden, und das gelingt nur gemeinsam, ausgehend von einer geteilten Haltung, einer gemeinsamen Alltagsrealität, einer soliden Vertrauensbasis, einem gemeinsamen Projekt für den Frieden.

Sicherheit ... ein Grundgefühl, die Basis für Frieden. Dafür brauche ich Gewissheiten für meinen Alltag, festen Boden für Kraft und Energie, Stützmauern für die Hände, klare Orientierungspunkte, geteilte Erinnerungen als Ausgangspunkt der Wege zu einer friedlichen Gesellschaft; die (gefühlte) Hoheit über das eigene Tun, über die unmittelbaren Alltagsbedingungen zu haben, eine Sprache, die Vertrauen schafft ... damit ich, damit wir gemeinsam die Steine wegräumen, die nächsten Tritte gehen können.

Freund*innen sind da, sie sind nahe, sie geben einander Sicherheit. Es ist das Vertraute, das Wissen nicht allein zu sein, das Wissen, dass auch morgen kein Alarm kommt, dass wir morgen saubere Luft atmen, gutes Essen, sauberes Wasser haben, arbeiten können. Wir brauchen die Sicherheit, dass wir unsere alltäglichen Bedürfnisse decken, uns treffen, austauschen, handeln können. Es ist die Sicherheit nicht allein zu sein ... das gibt die nötige Ruhe, Sicherheit, Stabilität, Vertrauen, als unverzichtbare Basis für Frieden.

What Makes Me Feel Safe

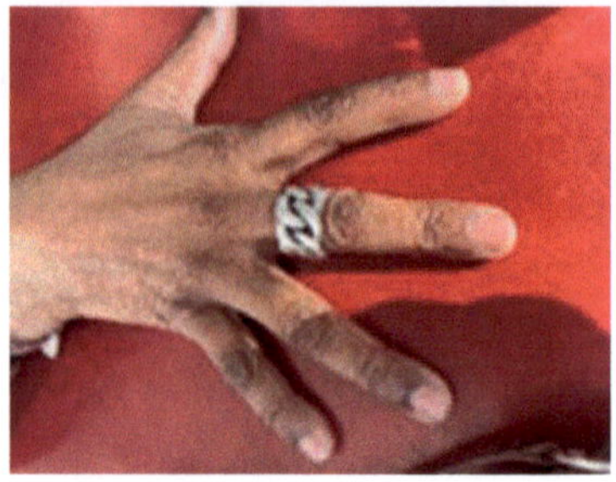

Theodora Leite Stampfli, *lawyer and migration specialist, moved to Switzerland from Brazil many years ago.*

Interview by **Annemarie Sancar**

Safe ... I feel safe when I feel good mentally, in my head. When I lived in Brazil as a young woman, there was so much crime, so much violence, everywhere, on the streets, in shops, but I always felt safe, also because I knew how to behave, how to move, where not to go. In short, I knew how to deal with it.

It is completely different here and the older I get, the more insecure I feel. It is not the material things that make me feel insecure, no, it is the emerging feeling of being a stranger, I often lack a sense of belonging and that makes me insecure. Friendships like with you or F. are important sources of safety for me. We have known each other for a long time, we have worked together, and we are familiar with each other. Once, very early on, you gave me something to read at work and asked for my opinion. I was perplexed, but of course delighted that you had so much trust in me. These moments give me a sense of security.

My safe haven? My two men at home, my son and my husband. They give me all the safety I need to feel at ease. When I come home, I take off my street or work clothes and go under the shower, sometimes I cry under the running water. That is how I wash my body and my soul, sometimes this is necessary. Then I feel good, I put on my „house clothes" and my slippers, I need that: And you know, my son, like me, he loves to stay at home in the „Roupa de casa". This term is like an agreement between the two of us, such things are sources of security to me. Something else: cooking at home, I'm not a good cook, but I love being creative, trying things out, that also gives me stability in life, cooking at home is part of it.

I was attacked and robbed four times in Brazil. Looking back, I think, no, I never felt insecure about it. I was not afraid. I knew how to behave. I knew how to assess the danger.

Recently I had to buy clothes for a very special occasion. The shop assistants here in Bern looked at me so contemptuously and with such condescension, they treated me like a ... or did I just feel like that this young woman treated me that way? One of them asked me cheekily, what are you doing here? My husband was behind me, he then asked if I knew this woman, as she had just called me by my first name. The shop assistant really flinched, she had not expected that ... a bit of satisfaction after the humiliation. That can still pull the rug out from under your feet, not always, but sometimes it happens to me, why is that, I ask myself? Alone in certain streets of Bern at night, I almost do not dare to walk on my own anymore. I have been mistaken for someone else and mobbed from time to time. Therefore, I hardly ever go out on the streets in the city at night, it is enough that you experience it once and your security disappears!

Safety ... there is my ring, I always wear it, it offers me protection, it is like a little amulet. I must never lose it. Sometimes I just sit in my room and look at my jewellery, just silver.

I often read. Nowadays, I only read novels in Portuguese, my mother tongue, which gives me the feeling of being at home, in a safe harbour – security, familiarity, a sense of security.

Was macht mich sicher

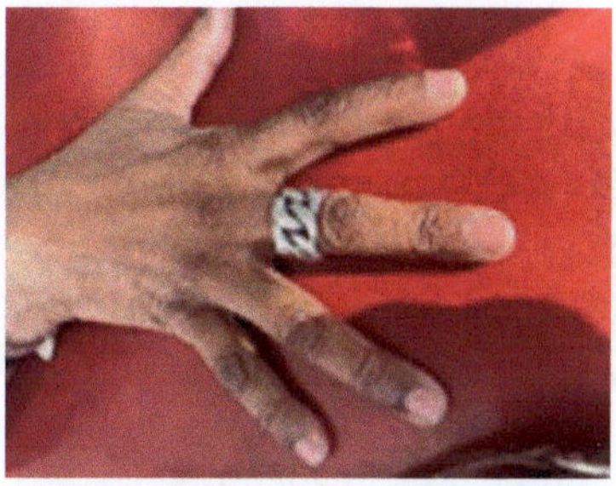

***Theodora Leite Stampfli**, Juristin und Migrationsfachfrau, vor vielen Jahren aus Brasilien in die Schweiz gekommen.*
*Interview von **Annemarie Sancar***

Sicher ... ich fühle mich sicher, wenn ich mich geistig, im Kopf wohl fühle. Als ich noch in Brasilien lebte, als junge Frau, da gab es ja so viele Kriminalität, soviel Gewalt, überall, auf den Strassen, in Geschäften, aber ich fühlte mich immer sicher, auch weil ich ja wusste wie ich mich verhalten soll, wie mich bewegen, wohin ich sicher nicht gehe. Kurz, ich wusste wie damit umzugehen.

Hier ist es ganz anders und je älter ich werde, desto unsicherer fühle ich mich hier. Es ist nicht das Materielle, das mich etwas unsicher machen würde, nein, es ist das aufkommende Gefühl fremd zu sein, mir fehlt oft Geborgenheit und das macht mich unsicher. Freundschaften wie mit dir oder F., das sich für mich wichtige Orte der Sicherheit. Wie kennen uns sehr lange, haben zusammengearbeitet, sind einander vertraut. Einmal, vor langer Zeit, hattest du mir bei der Arbeit etwas zum Lesen gegeben und um meine Meinung gebeten. Ich war perplex, aber vor Freude, dass du so viel Vertrauen in mich hattest. Dies Momente geben mir Sicherheit.

Mein sicherer Hafen? Das sind meine beiden Männer, mein Sohn und mein Ehemann. Sie geben mir alle Geborgenheit, die ich brauche um mich wohl zu fühlen. Wenn ich nach Hause komme, ziehe ich meine Strassen- oder Arbeitskleider aus, gehe unter die Douche, manchmal weine ich unter dem fliessenden Wasser. So wasche ich meinen Körper und meine Seele, manchmal ist das notwendig. Dann fühle ich mich gut, ich ziehe die «Hauskleider» über und meine Pantoffeln, das brauche ich, und weisst du, mein Sohn, der liebt es ebenso in der «Roupa de casa» zu Hause zu verweilen. Dieser Begriff ist wie eine Abmachung zwischen uns beiden, das sind eben dann so Dinge die mir Sicherheit geben. Auch das Kochen zuhause, ich bin zwar keine gute Köchin, liebe es aber kreativ zu sein, auszuprobieren, auch das gibt mir Halt im Leben.

In Brasilien wurde ich vier Mal überfallen, ausgeraubt. Rückblickend denke ich, nein, ich fühlte mich deswegen nie unsicher, ich wusste wie mich verhalten. Ich wusste die Gefahr einzuschätzen.

Vor kurzem musste ich für einen sehr besonderen Anlass Kleider kaufen. Die Verkäuferinnen hier in Bern, blickten mich so verächtlich und herablassend an, sie behandelten mich wie eine … oder fühlte ich mich einfach nur so behandelt? Eine fragte mich frech, was willst du eigentlich hier? Hinter mir war mein Mann, er fragte dann ob ich diese Frau denn kenne, wenn sich mich duzt. DA zuckte die Verkäuferin regelrecht zusammen, das hatte sie nicht erwartet … ein bisschen Genugtun nach der Demütigung? Das kann dennoch den Boden unter den Füssen wegziehen, nicht immer, aber manchmal passiert mir das, wieso das, frage ich mich? Nachts allein in bestimmten Strassen von Bern, das wage ich heute fast nicht mehr, ab und zu wurde ich verwechselt und angepöbelt, ich gehe kaum nachts in der Stadt auf die Strasse, es genügt, dass man es einmal erlebt und die Sicherheit schwindet!

Sicherheit … da ist mein Ring, ich trage ihn immer, er bietet mir Schutz, er ist wie ein kleines Amulett. Manchmal sitze ich in meinem Zimmer und betrachte meinen Schmuck, alles Silber. Oft lese ich. Romane lese ich heute nur noch auf Portugiesisch, das gibt mir das Gefühl zuhause zu sein, im sicheren Hafen – Geborgenheit, Vertrautheit.

What Makes Me Feel Safe

Constance Kaboré, *Burkina Faso, jurist and human rights (women's rights) activist, founder of ALIA (Association Action libre Afrique) in 2016 and recently organiser of a public library in a poor part of Ouagadougou*

I spent my childhood in no uncertain terms

Hearing the distant sounds of war

On television, on the radio, but nothing more

It only concerns other people, I thought.

Little by little, at the end of my primary school years, the war came closer.

In 2002, in Côte d'Ivoire, our neighbour had gone there for the holidays,

When the war started.

When I was 11, I had my first bout of insomnia.

This neighbour was my friend. What had happened to him? Could he have escaped?

I found out years later. Thank God, he had made it.

I saw thousands of Burkinabes who were expatriates,

coming back, fleeing that ivory land, their forgotten paradise.

I saw it on television, but it always seemed a bit far away.

Then came Mali ...

Which brought with it its share of refugees who saw Burkina Faso as an El Dorado...

The schools were occupied by fleeing Malians.

They were helped as much as possible...

I kept telling myself that Burkina had been spared.

But one day ...

A terrorist attack took place in a restaurant that I particularly liked for the quality of its meals.

It was 2016. I was 25 years old.

Since then, our country has never known a day of peace ...

I see thousands of people suffering ...

I see people I know suffering ...

I suffer ...

I have committed myself to the cause of peace, for women.

WOMEN! The great loser in every war.

Losing her children, her brothers, fathers and husbands.

Losing her dignity.

Losing her peace.

Widowed, they have to fight twice over.

Without a son, they no longer have the will to live.

And yet they are asked to live ...

For me, reading has always been the best way to escape.

What can I do but encourage you to do the same?

Immersed in a good book, you forget the sound of gunfire, you banish your sadness,

immerse yourself in a world of laughter or love,

a detective story or an everyday adventure.

In a good book, you learn to love, to tolerate, to cultivate the good.

I've set up a library. I encourage people to read. And I write.

I write about the distress of men. I describe the reality of women.

I do not forget the violated innocence of children ...

Peace. More than ever, our generation is looking for it.

More than ever, our world is looking for it.

More than ever, Constance KABORE is looking for it.

Constance Kaboré, *Burkina Faso, juriste et activste pour les droits humains et droits des femmes, fondatrice de ALIA (Association Action libre Afrique), fondée en 2016 et en 2023 créatrice d'une bibliothèque publique dans un quartier défavorisé de Ouagadougou*

J'ai vécu une enfance sans ambages

Entendant au loin des bruits de guerre

A télévision, à la radio, mais rien de plus

Ça ne concerne que les autres, pensais-je.

Peu à peu, à la fin de mon école primaire, la guerre se fit proche.

En 2002, en côte d'ivoire, notre voisin y était allé pour les vacances,

Quand la guerre y débuta.

A 11 ans, j'eus pour la 1ère fois des insomnies.

Ce voisin était mon ami. Que lui était-il arrivé ? Avais-t-il pu se sauver ?

Je le sus des années plus tard. Dieu merci, il avait pu s'en sortir.

Je vis des milliers de Burkinabès qui étaient expatriés,

Revenir en fuyant cette terre d'ivoire, leur paradis oublié.

Je voyais à la télévision, mais cela me semblait toujours un peu lointain.

Puis ce fut le Mali ...

Qui entraina son lot de réfugiés qui voyaient le Burkina comme un eldorado...

Les écoles étaient occupées par les maliens en fuite.

Ils étaient aidés autant que possible ...

Je me disais encore : le Burkina est épargné.

Mais, un jour...

Une attaque terroriste se fit dans un restaurant que j'affectionnais particulièrement pour la qualité de leurs repas.

En 2016. J'avais 25 ans ...

Depuis lors, notre pays n'a plus connu un jour de paix ...

Je vois des milliers de personnes qui souffrent...

Je vois mes connaissances souffrir...

Je souffre...

Je me suis engagée pour la cause de la paix, pour la femme.

LA FEMME ! Grande perdante dans chaque guerre.

Perdante de ses enfants, de ses frères, pères et époux.

Perdante de sa dignité.

Perdante de sa paix.

Veuves, elles doivent se battre doublement.

Sans fils, elles n'ont plus la volonté de vivre.

Et pourtant on leur demande de vivre...

La lecture a toujours été pour moi le meilleur moyen d'évasion.

Que puis-je faire sinon encourager à faire de même ?

Plongée dans un bon livre, tu oublies les bruits de fusil, tu chasses ta tristesse,

tu te plonges dans un monde de fous rires ou de d'amour,

dans une intrigue policière ou des aventures du quotidien.

Dans un bon livre, tu apprends à aimer, à tolérer, à cultiver le bien.

J'ai créé une bibliothèque. J'encourage à lire. A faire lire. Et j'écris.

J'écris la détresse des hommes. Je décris la réalité des femmes.

Je n'oublie pas l'innocence violée des enfants…

La Paix. Plus que jamais, notre génération la cherche.

Plus que jamais notre monde la cherche.

Plus que jamais, Constance KABORE la cherche.

Ouagadougou 15 octobre 2024

What Makes Me Feel Safe

Oleksandra Zinenko, Picture 1 for Voices along the Way

Olena Zinenko, *Ukraine, university lecturer in Charkiw and Frankfurt/Oder, cultural activist, media practitioner. Anita Augsburg Award winner WILPF Germany*

My sense of security is about being able to stay in touch. In the autumn of 2022, I was in Lviv during the shelling. The power turn off, and half an hour later, the internet was cut off. And then I felt some signs of panic, because I realised that, firstly, I had no access to the news, and secondly, I could not call my loved ones. In addition, I couldn't charge my phone because I forgot the charger in the hotel room. What gave me a sense of security at that moment? My knowledge and responsibility for people, because I had to lead a training on those days, and I knew I had to be composed and not panic. They also gave me a sense of support, especially when they agreed that we should continue the training by candlelight.

Олена Зіненко

Моє відчуття безпеки стосується можливості бути на зв'язку. Восені 2022 року, я опинилася у Львові під час обстрілу. Вимкнули світло, а за півгодини – інтернет. І тут я відчула якісь ознаки паніки, бо зрозуміла, що, по-перше, не маю доступу до новин, по-друге, не можу подзвонити своїм близьким. Окрім того, я не можу зарядити телефон, бо забула зарядку в готельному номері. Що мені давало відчуття безпеки в той момент? Мої знання та відповідальність за людей, бо я в ці дні мала вести тренінг, і знала, що маю поводитися зібрано і не панікувати. Вони також мені надали відчуття підтримки, особливо коли погодилися на те, щоб ми продовжували тренінг при свічах.

What Makes Me Feel Safe

***Nata Kogan**, mother of Olena Zinenko.*

Since the beginning of the full-scale Russian invasion of Ukraine, I have been in Kharkiv. I heard all the attacks on my city, the bombs and rockets that exploded a kilometre away from my house. At the beginning, I was wrong because of my usual anger and borsch, or rather the smell of borsch, a Ukrainian folk dish. Later, I realised that the feeling of safety for me was the understanding that I was not alone, that there were Kharkivites, my big community, who would organise themselves and pull me out of the rubble, bring me food, clothes, and find a place to live. I saw these people when I went out on the streets. When there was no light in the winter, in the evening people would put lanterns on their heads and walk around like fireflies. During the day, the city was filled with the sounds of generators that kept shops, cafes, banks, etc. open. It gives me a sense of security.

Ната Коган.

З початку повномасштабного вторгнення РФ в Україну я знаходжуся у Харкові. Я чула усі атаки на моє місто, як розривалися бомби і ракети, що падали в кілометрі від мого дому. В перші роки мене рятувала звичайна злість та борщ, точніше запах борщу – української народної страви. Пізніше я відчула, що відчуття безпеки для мене – це розуміння, що я не одна, є харків'яни, моя громада, які, будь що, організуються і витягнуть мене з-під завалів, принесуть їжу, одяг, знайдуть де жити. Я бачила цих людей, коли виходила на вулиці. Коли не було світла взимку, ввечорі люди вдягали ліхтарики на голову і так ходили, наче світлячки. Вдень місто наповнювалося звуками генераторів, які забезпечували роботу магазинів, кав'ярень, банків тощо. Це надавало мені відчуття безпеки.

What Makes Women Feel Safe

Eliko Bendeliani, *Chair of the Center for Peace and Civic Development, experiencing participation and peace building of (young) women*

Our security today is uncertain. But the question goes beyond security: how do we see our future? For us, that future is undeniably linked to Europe. We are a traumatised society that understands the struggles of its past and broadly supports our European aspirations. The Georgian society is very traumatised and the Russian war against Ukraine has intensified this feeling. In our political landscape, we face the manipulation of the term „peace" by various parties, often in ways that contradict our vision. As young women activists, the quest for sustainable peace remains vital, and we emphasise the concept of, common security' to counteract pervasive fears. Many fear that Georgia could be the next target after Ukraine, making both possible outcomes of the war – either a Ukrainian victory or a Russian one – dangerous for us. In addition, we recognise the geostrategic power games that impede democratic stability and development while serious negotiations are still ongoing.

Being only observers in this „game" makes us rather weak and paralyses activities. As civil society, we need platforms to discuss and learn from each other, from neighbouring countries as well as from our European and international partners and sisters. The recent law against foreign agents only shrinks and destroys this (educational) space. Building common security between Georgia and Armenia is a complex but important task to ensure our security, especially as the youth aspire to such a goal. It requires careful management of historical grievances, geopolitical alignments and economic interests. Focus on areas of mutual benefit, such as economic cooperation.

„Peacing the Peace" Conference in Yerevan, Armenia 2024

„Building common security between Georgia and Armenia is a complex but important task to ensure our security, especially as the youth aspire to such a goal. It requires careful management of historical grievances, geopolitical alignments and economic interests. By focusing on areas of mutual benefit such as economic cooperation, human security and regional stability, and by fostering trust through dialogue and confidence-building measures, the two countries can work towards a more secure and stable relationship. However, the success of such efforts will depend on the political will of each country's leadership, the influence of external powers, and the ability to address the underlying issues that have historically divided the two nations". The **Youth Peace and Security Agenda/YPS** contains many elements that we can draw on.

We are highly motivated to continue our struggle. When I go to a conflict-affected region and meet with people there, I notice that there are more women in the meetings. They are always proactive; they bravely discuss ways to solve problems. But in practice they are limited to working on technical issues rather than being directly involved in the process.

However, there are successful examples of women's involvement in peace initiatives that are unfortunately not well known to the public. Traditionally, they have been reluctant to speak out, fearing that publicising the process could undermine the outcome. In recent years, however, women have done much to build confidence and have made valuable contributions to the peace process through their own activities.

Today, the biggest problem for young women on different sides of the conflict is the lack of direct communication channels. Those working for peace are very active, but they have never had direct communication. Social media is a good opportunity, but it is also full of challenges. The problem is that the people who are most active in the digital space are those with negative and aggressive attitudes, who are not willing to contribute to the effective implementation of peace processes.

On our side, the problem is a lack of in-depth information, which is often evident in meetings, so I think it is important to acquire more knowledge, formulate structure opinions and critically rethink existing perceptions.

It is also worth noting that the young people involved in the negotiations do not know each other and have no experience of living together. Unfortunately, there was a period after the conflict when communication between communities was minimal. Then, as new generations emerged, the estrangement increased and the need to overcome it became apparent.

Systematic work on women's empowerment is very important. Women's roles need to be recognised - and civil, political and economic empowerment initiatives need to be supported. At the same time, in order to ensure women's political participation, there is a need for targeted interventions and the implementation of projects aimed at their participation in political and social processes.

In my opinion, the most important thing today is to prove to women that they are confident and that they can make a difference. They have the potential to create a different, peaceful and socio-political agenda. They need more opportunities in the political arena to become real decision-makers, and their participation should not be merely symbolic or a façade.

Young people from different groups perceive the issue of conflict differently. For those living along the dividing lines, the issue is one of daily security, and for the internally displaced, it is one of feelings that affect their lives to varying degrees – so their motivation tends to be higher at times.

In general, the younger generation is the notable part of society that is most interested in receiving in-depth information and has a greater willingness to listen to different narratives.

This is evident in the growing demand for courses, programmes and training on conflict and peace processes. There is a great desire on the part of young, successful people working in different institutions to fill the information vacuum and get involved in these processes. This is very important, because if we do not work together on a solution, it will be difficult to make progress to feel safe!

What makes me Feel Safe

Gulnara Shahinian, *„Democracy Today" Founder and Director, UN Special Rapporteur on Slavery 2008-2015*

Safety for me is about stability. It means being surrounded by friends I trust and respect, staying well-connected. As I've grown older, I've become more selective about the people I keep close. My small inner circle consists of those I've learned from and respected over the years, which gives me a sense of security.

Throughout my life, especially when pioneering uncomfortable subjects, I have often felt unsafe. For example, I conducted the first-ever research on human trafficking in the UAE and other countries, or started my mandate on slavery – something most people thought was long abolished and no longer needed discussion. These were not easy tasks, but the knowledge that my work could save lives made me feel safe, even amid threats and real danger. I felt secure because I knew what I was doing, and most importantly, why I was doing it. I've always prioritized the safety and wellbeing of others, even when it was not entirely allowed. That sense of responsibility made me strong.

The only time I felt truly vulnerable was when I realized people were lying. That's a situation where safety feels compromised.

I was born in Georgia, as an Armenian in the Soviet Republic, where many of my relatives were exiled, imprisoned, or disappeared during Stalin's regime in 1937. Being part of a minority meant that I couldn't study where I wanted. They wanted to send me to North Ossetia, but my parents refused. Instead, I moved to Yerevan to attend university, and later, after getting married, I moved to Moscow with my husband, who was working on his dissertation in theoretical physics. Although we were offered the chance to stay in Moscow, we never felt it was our spiritual home and decided to return to Yerevan.

Back in Yerevan, I began working in the City Council's Department of Foreign Affairs during a crucial time. Armenia was taking its first steps toward independence from the Soviet Union, and the atmosphere was charged with excitement and hope. I witnessed people rallying in the streets, reciting forbidden poetry, singing songs of freedom – it was an inspiring and incredible sight. However, this time of hope was quickly followed by hardship: war broke out between Armenia and Azerbaijan, thousands of refugees flooded into Armenia, and the devastating earthquake claimed 25,000 lives. On top of that, a blockade imposed by Turkey left Armenia without basic necessities for nearly two years.

Despite all this, Armenia's resolve toward independence and democracy didn't waver. Women played a critical role during this time, especially when Russian troops arrived to suppress the movement. In Armenia, women understood that the soldiers were often young boys who didn't even know where they were. Women baked cookies and brought them to the soldiers, trying to show them kindness amidst the chaos.

Under the patronage of the First Lady, we organized the first women's conference in Armenia, „Armenian Women at the Doorstep of the 21st Century," to highlight the significant role women played in the independence movement. It was an exciting yet challenging time to be part of this transformation.

Later, I became the only woman elected as Deputy Mayor of Yerevan, working alongside 13 men. It was a learning experience in finding my voice and ensuring that issues particularly important to women were addressed. I eventually transitioned to working with the International Organization for Migration (IOM), which led me to an even more challenging role: becoming the first UN Special Rapporteur on Contemporary Forms of Slavery.

This mandate, while honorary and unpaid, was incredibly complex. No state wanted to admit to having slavery. They could acknowledge human trafficking but refused to see slavery within their borders. I found myself standing not just against criminals but also government officials who benefited from modern slavery. Yet, I persisted, determined to expose and address these realities. In Haiti, for example, I spoke out against the exploitation of child domestic laborers, known as restaveks, despite facing intense opposition from those in power.

There were successes, too. In Mauritania, where even mentioning the word „slavery" was forbidden, I managed to convince the President to acknowledge its existence and develop laws to protect those escaping slavery. Women, in particular, suffered greatly, often used as laborers, given as dowry, and even gifted to others. Breaking the societal stigma around slavery was a massive challenge, but necessary for change.

In Ecuador, I had to flee from criminals while working on issues of child exploitation in gold mines. These children were forced to wash gold in mercury-contaminated water, which devastated their health and the environment. Despite the dangers, I documented what I saw and brought the evidence before the Human Rights Council.

Throughout my career, safety – both mine and that of the people I was helping – was deeply interconnected. Many times, I received threats to leave countries immediately, but my mission was always to raise awareness and find solutions. My goal was to protect these vulnerable people without putting them in further danger after I left.

In Armenia, through my organization „Democracy Today," we've worked to help women, youth, and refugees, particularly in border regions. Our work promotes peace and democracy in a country that has faced incredible challenges. My team is like an extended family, built on trust and respect, which gives me a profound sense of security.

Despite the turbulence in Armenia, we remain committed to supporting peace and democracy. Democracy Today serves as a catalyst for collaboration among activists, public leaders, and scholars. We take a comprehensive approach, involving stakeholders at all levels to nurture communities that are empowering, equitable, and resilient. This is what gives me hope and safety: the knowledge that peace and democracy can be achieved through perseverance and collective effort.

What Makes Me Feel Safe

Nora Ahmetaj, *Kosovo, peace consultant in transitional justce, reconciliation and right to truth for the victims, currently mandated by Civil Peace Corps Germany*

How and why do I feel safe, what makes me feel insecure and what are the remedies, what are my strategies for creating the feeling of safety?

The sense of being secure, I believe, changes with age. My name is Nora, and I am Albanian from Kosovo. As young people full of dreams and emotions, we think that being safe is what we were told as children, which is to have a healthy family and to trust it above all else. Family gives you the feeling of security. But over time, you realize that the family nucleus, as we were raised to believe, provides a kind of security, especially if we come from places where institutions are fragile and do not have a real contract with the citizen. Therefore, citizens turn back to their families, especially women, without considering that the sense of being offered ‚security' by the family also gives it the right to manage or command the way of life. This is particularly reflected in women when they get married and do not have economic autonomy; the family then transforms into an agency where, under the provision of shelter, it discriminates, exploits, manages your life, and in situations where you are disobedient, it may even maltreat or take your life. I made this observation to show that family is not necessarily the main shield. As a child, I was told to learn and become independent. Much later, I began to understand that my parents knew something when they told us that only economic independence and education could offer us a more comfortable life. When the first political upheavals began in the 80s in Kosovo (the part of the Former Yugoslavia), I was a 10-year-old child, and I couldn't yet see that the entire trajectory of my life and education would go in the direction dictated by socio-political conditions, and later also economic ones. When I turned 18, Miloševic was already established in power, and at the time when I started studying architecture, I thought my dream would come true; instead, we were forcefully expelled from the university and left on the streets, while our parents lost their jobs because they were Albanians and turned disobedient towards dictatorship rules. I see this difficult political and economic situation as the biggest turning point in my life, as I had no choice but to turn towards the future in the conflictual situation that prevailed. Therefore, I began to take an interest in what was happening around me and why. At that time, it was crucial for me to be alive and healthy; my security and that of my compatriots was existential, life or death. With the end of the war in Kosovo, even though we who survived thought we had overcome a great challenge and survived, as long as we were breathing, it gave us hope that we as people would try to improve the socio-economic situation. At 30, you are full of dreams and ambitions; therefore, at that time, I saw security as something that offered me freedom of movement that I did not have as a Kosovar (since we were not allowed to travel without visas anywhere in the West). I had a job but wanted to travel, to buy an apartment, and I saw all these materials things as achievable since, first and foremost, I had the freedom to breathe freely. Over time, and as the years went by, I saw that human needs were not limited to just ambitions, but we needed social peace, security in accessing work as a woman, the assurance of equal treatment, the security to speak with your own voice, and to be disobedient in a society that thinks that the woman should be obedient. As the years passed and ambitions changed shape, so too did the perception and need to feel safe take on different forms and shapes. Over time, I realized that human security guaranteed me health security, security to have a dignified old age, security to live in a society where, as a woman, I am not stigmatized but praised for the courage I had to choose to live alone, security to have stable employment and not to be discriminated against during hiring on the basis of age. These became the conditions that I saw and still see today as giving me security. I also think of security when my neighbors surrounding my state are democratic and constructive, so that I do not feel insecure in this life as if I would experience another war. Security would also come from the fact that this world has fewer wars, as they also affect our well-being both economically and mentally. In a world full of political and economic turbulence, injustice, and inequality, the phrase „work locally but think globally" makes a lot of sense. But I also cannot find comfort in being privileged because I have health insurance, a pension retirement trust, or a solid job when I know that all this will be lost the moment my life is insecure due to various global factors. Therefore, while we are part of the earthly globe, our individual well-being should not be taken for granted, as I see everything as interlinked and interdependent. Thus, let's work locally to make the world around us more secure.

What Makes Me Feel Safe

Andrea Marikovszky, *Hungary, artist, performer, teacher, art therapist, social worker, universalist against the banality of violence*

Humour and creativity helps me to survive the violence that I experience in many forms, many obvious and hidden ways, day after day. The banality of the different form of violences make us slowly believe that violence is normal, it should not be even called violence, but better to see it as the nature of normal human beings.

I do not want to think like this.

For me art is a form of resistance to this way of thinking.

I also do art as a remedy which cures the experience of being neglected, ignored and exploited. It allows me to experience myself as being a valued citizen, in such a society that wants to use and exploit me as a woman and as a worker, but does not want to support my fulfilment as a living human being and feel myself as being a valued human being. Appreciation is only for the money and status elite and the stars in neolibereal capitalism.

We will no longer be Muses – 2018 – Photographer: Sonja Zámbó

The common illusion of the regime change in 1989 in Hungary, that one can be anyone, because everybody is free to chose its destiny, has vanished a longtime ago. The reality of capitalism is a hierarchy of status, rivalry with each other, black labour and precarious work, no idea for the future, alienation, objectification of the other person, no social mobility, selfish competition, lack of material conditions for self-fulfilment, and last but not least, the reinforcement of patriarchal values and the arming.

Hungary is a post-socialist country in central Europe, a colony of the Austrian Monarchy until 1918, then part of Nazi Germany, and it became under Russian occupation from 1945 to 1991, with Soviet troops stationed here, mandatory conscription, and ruined military barracks to this day.

In 1989 we had the illusion that the change of regime, after socialism had brought independence to the country. But in fact the country never had true socialism, even though all the social benefits and welfare measures that still exist today, such as family allowances and two years' childcare leave after birth, were created in that socialist era. It is more accurate to call this period of the state capitalism regime, where a political elite ruled by frying its own bacon. But still had the value of collectivity and solidarity in the society.

We will be heroes again – 2018 – Photographer: Sonja Zámbó

So in the last 30 years, this system has been changed into a semi-peripheral version neo-liberal capitalism. It came upon us as a result of the people's longing for the Western consumer culture, not thinking or knowing about the disappointing consequences of individualism, and the dismantling of the role of the state. We would never have dreamed that Western people would flock to Hungary, buy apartments and lands for peanuts, and then run them for example airB&B while we couldn't afford to rent flats and buy flats for ourselves and for our children without getting ourselves hopelessly into debt. It obviously makes the base for xenophobia.

In this summer 2024, over my 50 years, with three university diplomas and low teacher's salary, I am going to clean some of these flats for a black payment of 3000 Ft (6 euros) per apartment. No one cares that I'm too qualified to clean for a living.

These owners who obviously don't pay taxes in this country - and anyway I do not see much from the taxes in general - as I clean their precious belongings for black money, obviously don't think of themselves as capitalists and exploiters. It is just good to realize that the former well known form of colonialism has become so hidden by today. We, Hungarians, specially women, serve the interest of small and big capitalists, national and multinational businesses, or go to western countries as elderly people's care workers often overqualified for the job, as we have created national big-capital meadows by squandering the public wealth of the Hungarian socialist era.

Hungary by today leads the way in extreme inequalities by squandering of the commons and after 30 years of system change, it has become one of the the poorest country in Europe. We work a lot, earn little, and fear of loosing even these little black money which make us feel safer, and able to give a European life style for our children.

In Hungary, the status hierarchy is a very powerful determinant of people's thinking and behaviour. So what is worth, is constantly priced in. Being a mother is symbolically very valuable. However, financially this ‚recognition' of mothers – connected to the christian cultus of Mary - is not manifested. If a person becomes a mother without having had before a job with status and long term contract - which is often the case, as employers employ the majority on temporary, casual contracts, or without any contracts at all -, she receives 28,500 HUF (71 euro) per month for three years. To this is added the family allowance of 12,500 (31 euro) HUF per child per month. This amount has not changed for more than 15 years, despite the inflation of money on numerous occasions. Single mothers – like me - receive 13,500 HUF (34 euro), which means that the state only gives 1,000 HUF (3 euro) more to those who have children in a single-earner family. The general wage around 1000 euro, and the food mostly costs more than in Austria or other western countries.

So it is not an exaggeration to say: Hungarians have become cheap labour in the global capitalist labour market. Today we are now oppressed not by other nations but by the global and local capital and by ourselves. It is important to emphesise: this was the result of the 1989 regime change. This made it possible to change the ethical values of socialistic ideas about collectivism to a free market capitalist ideas, when everything and everyone became for sale in the world of market. Despite digitalisation, we are working more and more for less and less money.

Those women who take up motherhood are risking certain impoverishment in Hungary. Teachers, artists, women do a huge amount of undignified work below their skills and qualifications in this digital capitalism era. What is this if not a daily experience of the banality of violence?

I belong to the generation of the Hungarian regime change, I became eligible to vote in 1988, so I was able to vote for the first time in the first multi-party elections of the regime change. The country in which I live since that and I am the mother of three children - in the words of Nancy Fraser - operates on the same cannibalistic capitalist principles as most countries today. It denies the background jobs and resources that are the basis of its existence and survival. It does not repay women's caring, emotional, social reproductive work, but takes it for granted, just as it takes nature for granted, into which it only puts back the rubbish and pollution, without putting its cycles before its own interests.

Hungary is a country of „chocolates". We can pretend how nice and good everything is. We are ashamed to admit our failures and difficulties, and since the 1956 revolution, the revolution defeated by the Russians and not saved by the Western countries or USA, we have been almost incapable of saying enough is enough. Our relationships and our workplaces are defined by conformity, by the way conflicts are handled, by repression of ourselves, and a deep respect for the bosses. We love authoritarian, specially male leaders who always tell us which way is up. Because of this, the Hungarian people pretend a lot, while digging in their heels. But maybe this is not a Hungarian situation, but a characteristic of the self-made-(wo)man characters bred by capitalist societies based on rivalry and status hierarchies.

My pictures are my way of saying, here you go with your self-made-woman, fck off! The new-old system promised us it would be good, and I can do it. It promised every human being can fulfill itself if we eliminate the paternalistic care of the state. By now I know that the capitalist system just has left us with the task of caring, just left us to solve it without costing to it anything. And while we impoverish ourselves and become invisible under the carpet of unpaid, underpaid and invisible work, a spectacle will be built in which everything is too good and too beautiful. But the reality behind the spectacle shop window world there is rot, wheat and death. We are not self-made, but determined by gender, race and age, and locality, and by where we can be used in the global production and care chain.

All photos are taken from the series @SELF@MADE@WOMAN Andrea Marikovszky, 2015 - 2018

A limited numbered edition, signed and numbered by the artist is available for sale posted in a hard backed photography form in 50 cm x 70 cm, 70 cm x 100 cm and 95cm x 135 cm.

Order: andrea.marikovszky@gmail.com

Women, read every day!
2018 – Photographer: Sonja Zámbó

Read every day and be useless, women! Care only for your own humanistic value, not for serving profit. This will be your future and your real freedom in a future of solidarity that puts human and nature beings before profit.

My artistic works are at once sad and humorously grotesque, reflecting on these problems of Hungarian women, where you can be a muse, a femme fatale, but you can not be a valued member of the society.

My series called Women, read every day! encourages women to take on the revolutionary task of acquiring their own knowledge and awakening their consciousness, spending useless time for their own good.

I created these photo-performances in a country where, despite the many disadvantages and violance that women have to face, feminism has been preserved and still important, even if only for a few dozen women, for decades. This land of sufferings has to be saved, has to be changed, women have to come out of self-colonisation.

What Makes Me Feel Safe

Florina Tufescu, *Romania, translator, member of World Beyond War and WILPF.*

I've never felt unsafe except in my childhood. I was born in 1977 in Romania, at a time of deep poverty, repression and fear. I learnt not to speak freely to anyone outside the family at the same time as I was learning how to speak. It was a necessary kind of teaching in a country held hostage by a nationalist dictator and by the Securitate, where a moment of innocent sharing could have landed my family in trouble or even in prison. So I learnt how to keep things to myself and how to pretend early on: in society, with my friends, but also with my family who were trying so hard to offer us a happy and secure childhood. Which of course, they couldn't, not entirely, since children inhabit the same world as the rest of us although they can escape it a bit more often thanks to a livelier and not yet disheartened imagination.

I've never felt unsafe since the end of December 1989, when the dictatorship came to an end, quite unexpectedly for me and perhaps for most Romanians. The whole web of distrust and guilty complicities, the disdain for democracy, for culture and for individual rights, which had dominated and shaped our society for decades, none of this vanished into thin air, of course, although for a very short while it seemed to us, to me at least, that it had. Soon enough I realised how naïve I'd been and that the rebuilding of Romania would entail a long and painful process, largely due to the powerful, if less visible, presence of the Securitate and communist party elite and their relentless dissemination of anti-democratic ideas and beliefs.

But at least I've felt safe since then. Safe to speak my mind, to make friends without reservations, to travel and study wherever I wish. Beauty and truth, science and art, love and friendship, have kept me safe. Wherever and however I may find myself, I feel accompanied by all of these and by their various signifiers in object form. Since I have to pick just one object that makes me feel safe, I will pick my friend's diary.

She gave it to me unexpectedly at the end of high school, when we knew we'd be living in different cities, far away from each other. Emma's diary shows self-insight and courage and contains my story too, of that time, as I could not have written it. I've returned to it after all these years and keep re-reading it in the hope that I can memorise the essential so that it is never lost. The essential about me and about her. „Always remember who you are“ as another friend once told me- or perhaps „always remember who you'd like to be“ may well be the ultimate place of safety.

But the essential about that diary is perhaps friendship itself- quite possibly the most extraordinary of all human inventions. Friendship which gives us the courage to see ourselves as we really are at a particular moment in time, but also the confidence that we can evolve beyond that, towards a finer version of ourselves. Friendship which can only take place between human beings, friendship which makes us feel safe, an oasis that exists within the real world, just a phone call or an e-mail away, a prototype version of what the world as a whole could eventually look like…

What Makes Me Feel Safe

Brigitte Obermayer, *Internationale Frauenliga für Frieden und Freiheit IFFF Deutschland*

International League for Peace and Freedom WILPF Germany

Alles, was Menschen brauchen, steht seit Urzeiten fest.

Viele kluge Menschen haben die Nachhaltigkeitsziele der UN definiert und weiterentwickelt.

Das Wissen ist da.

Es fehlt die Umsetzung.

Und wichtig sind Kunst und Kultur.

The real needs of people are clear since ever.

Many clever people have defined the Sustainable Development Goals of the UN.

The knowledge is there.

What is missing is implementation.

And art and culture are important.

What Makes Me Feel Safe

Heidi Meinzolt, *member of WILPF and coordinator in the Women&Gender working-group of the Civic Solidarity Platform/CSP in the OSCE area.*

Of course, the best thing is when I can sit in the garden on a warm summer day: It is quiet, flowers around me, birds singing, a marvellous luxury that gives me a momentary feeling of security, calm and contentment. I'm healthy, I'm not in need,, I can think critically and express myself, I have a wonderful family, good friends, curiosity and plans.

I was lucky: I never had to leave home, but I was always allowed to go out into the world.

Job bans had been abolished, so a close affinity to left-wing/even communist ideas, which was attested to by the authorities, nevertheless allowed me a career as a civil servant until I retired. Some students already understood what you can and must do with a conscious life. I was only confronted with a violent assault once on a school trip when I was attacked by a gang of girls. Women's self-defence didn't help me against the blows, which I tried to avoid by de-escalating – but that was as far as it went.

I had been involved in the local peace initiative since the beginning of my studies, in the 70s/80s against the rearmament with Pershing missiles at large demonstrations. I lived for an open Europe of the regions, understood security as a common task, strengthened by non-violent training. A variety of encounters in and with the global South – whether with a school exchange programme with Burkina Faso or with phantastic WILPF women – gave this a meaning.

After a few years of alternative living in the countryside, thoughts about preserving the ecological balance, a resource-conserving way of life, criticism of growth and the threat to the planet came to the centre of my perception and brought me into the Green Party in 1983, which in its early days as the anti-party party of Petra Kelly lived the synergy of ecological, peaceful, feminist and democratic elements. This also gave me the certainty that problems could be solved holistically, with good will and political participation. However, with the 'We are somebody again' of German reunification and a nation being defended in the Hindu Kush and bombing Serbia, the departure from party political work was inevitable. This interpretation of realpolitik no longer had anything to do with security as I understood it.

While I now look relaxed at the splendour of the flowers in the garden, uncertainty quickly spreads: aren't the bluebells symbolic of the alarm bells that I can hear ringing so loudly and clearly? What kind of absurd logic is spreading with the 'turn of an era'? I can also sense the fear of war, violence and the oppressive end of freedom and prosperity in my immediate surroundings. The crises of recent years – from Covid to environmental problems – and above all the wars and monstrous atrocities in Ukraine, Sudan and the Middle East, which we see every day as 'spectators', are leaving their mark. But not to the extent that we need to do more specifically for peace and climate justice. No, the lie that we need to become 'ready for war' for our own safety is spreading like a cancer and declaring our historically grown analysis of the women's peace movement, practised pacifism and/or anti-militarism to be naive and simply wrong.

But it is precisely the other way round: the mental, moral and unprecedented actual armament with the most modern weapons and a destructive potential for the whole world is taking away our security – even if the aeroplane above my head is not (yet) carrying bombs, but probably only tourists.

This is precisely why concern for the well-being of people/humanity and care remains a primary mission for me to set out the pathqays to peace every day, with small and sometimes very big steps – against all resistance from the mainstream.

Was macht mich sicher

***Heidi Meinzolt**, Mitglied der Internationalen Frauenliga für Frieden und Freiheit und Koordinatorin der Women&Gender Arbeitsgruppe der Civic Solidarity Platform/CSP in der OSZE.*

Am schönsten ist es natürlich, wenn ich mich an einem warmen Sommertag in den Garten setzen kann: Ruhe, Blumen, Vögel, ein grandioser Luxus, der mir ein momentanes Gefühl von Sicherheit, Ruhe und Zufriedenheit verleiht. Ich bin gesund, leide keine Not, kann kritisch denken und mich äußern, habe eine wunderbare Familie, gute Freund*innen, Neugier und Pläne.

Ich habe Glück gehabt: musste nie von zuhause weg, aber durfte eigentlich immer hinaus in die Welt.

Berufsverbote waren abgeschafft, so war mir trotz einer dienstlich attestierten Nähe zu linken/ ja kommunistischen Gedanken eine Beamtenkarriere bis zur Pensionierung möglich. Einige Schüler*innen haben schon verstanden, was man aus einem bewussten Leben machen kann und muss. Mit einem gewalttätigen Übergriff war ich nur einmal auf einer Schulfahrt durch den Angriff einer Mädchengang konfrontiert, da half mir die Frauenselbstverteidigung nichts gegen die Schläge, die ich mit Deeskalation vermeiden wollte – aber dabei blieb es auch.

Ich habe mich seit Studienbeginn in der lokalen Friedensinitiative engagiert, in den 70er/80er Jahren gegen die Nachrüstung mit Pershing-Raketen auf großen Demos. Ich lebte für ein offenes Europa der Regionen, verstand Sicherheit als gemeinsame Aufgabe, gestärkt durch gewaltfreies Training. Vielfältige Begegnungen im und mit dem globalen Süden – ob mit einem Schulaustausch mit Burkina Faso oder bei der Liga gaben dem einen Sinn.

Mit einigen Jahren alternativen Lebens auf dem Land, gerieten Gedanken zum Erhalt des ökologischen Gleichgewichts, einer ressourcenschonende Lebensweise, Wachstumskritik und die Gefährdung des Planeten ins Zentrum meiner Wahrnehmung und haben mich 1983 in die grüne Partei gebracht, die in der Anfangszeit als Anti-Parteien-Partei einer Petra Kelly das Zusammenspiel von ökologisch, friedlich, feministisch, demokratischen Elementen lebte. Auch das verlieh eine Sicherheit, dass Probleme ganzheitlich zu lösen wären, mit gutem Willen und politischer Partizipation. Mit dem „Wir sind wieder wer“ der deutschen Wiedervereinigung und einer Nation, die am Hindukusch verteidigt wird und Serbien bombardiert, war der Abschied aus der parteipolitischen Arbeit jedoch programmiert. Diese Interpretation von Realpolitik hatte nichts mehr mit der Sicherheit wie ich sie verstand zu tun.

Während ich nun so zunächst entspannt in die Blumenpracht im Garten schaue, macht sich doch schnell Verunsicherung breit: sind die Glockenblumen nicht symbolisch für die Alarmglocken, deren Sturmgeläute ich gerade so laut und deutlich vernehme? Was für eine absurde Logik macht sich mit der „Zeitenwende“ breit? Auch in meiner nächsten Umgebung spüre ich die Angst vor Krieg, Gewalt und auch dem beklemmenden Ende von Freiheit und Wohlstand. Die Krisen der letzten Jahre – von Covid bis zu Umweltproblemen - und vor allem die Kriege und ungeheuren Grausamkeiten in der Ukraine, im Sudan und im Nahen Osten, die wir täglich als „Zuschauer*innen“ wahrnehmen, hinterlassen Spuren. Aber nicht dahin, dass wir ganz konkret mehr für den Frieden und für Klimagerechtigkeit tun müssten. Nein, die Lüge, dass wir zu unserer Sicherheit „kriegstüchtig“ werden müssten, macht sich wie ein Krebsgeschwür breit und erklärt unsere historisch gewachsene Analyse der Frauen-Friedensbewegung, den praktizierten Pazifismus und/oder Anti-Militarismus für naiv und schlichtweg falsch.

Aber es ist doch gerade anders: Die geistig-moralische und lange nicht mehr dagewesene Aufrüstung mit den modernsten Waffen und einem Zerstörungspotential für die ganze Erde nimmt uns doch gerade die Sicherheit – auch wenn das Flugzeug über meinem Kopf (noch) keine Bomben trägt, sondern wohl nur Touristen.

Gerade deshalb bleibt für mich die Sorge um das Wohl der Menschen/der Menschheit ein primärer Auftrag, mich täglich auf den Weg zum Frieden zu machen, mit kleinen und manchmal ganz großen Schritte – gegen alle Widerstände aus dem Mainstream.

What Makes Me Feel Safe

Mariana Lechterbeck, *Co-President of the German section of the Women's International League for Peace and Freedom (WILPF), August 2024*

A lot has to do with how I grew up. Safe. Sheltered. Incredibly privileged in many ways. And with lots of music. Music feels like home. A place that is safe, especially because of the lovely people around me. I remember beautiful jazz sounds at the breakfast table in the morning. I remember anti-fascist and domestic violence awareness songs by "die Ärzte" (German popular band), the "Kinderlied" (transl. "children's song) by Joy Denalane (German musician, writing songs in German, English, Xhosa and Tsonga) my mom sang to me so often and her favorite song by Joy "Wem gehört die Welt" (transl. "Who owns the world) about racism and sexism and about the possibility of still being able to change the world. I remember my mom's great, loud, and confident voice (which of course stood out from all the other voices on every occasion and was incredibly embarrassing for me at 14 hihi), but also that we often cried together to music in difficult times. I think of many car journeys with my dad where we dreamed together to music. I think of autumn afternoons when the gentle sounds of my dad's piano lured me into the living room, and I could just listen. I think of spontaneous jam sessions with the whole family, of choir workshops and my little siblings, who were fascinated and enthusiastic about music from such a young age, of my dad's wife, who always sings to herself, even on the toilet, and my dad, who hums lots of groovy, self-rhymed nonsense songs in the morning to give us all a good start to the day. As a small child, I remember falling asleep on benches next to loud jukeboxes in pubs many times because my dad had a gig, in my head, I have endless images of my dad at keyboards and lost in the intoxication of music. And then, of course, I think a lot about how I make music. How often I sat crying at the piano and first let off my anger with loud and angry hammer chords and then calm myself down again with very soft melancholy sounds. Losing yourself in the sounds of the music you make is a wonderful, fascinating, safe feeling. I know that music feels so familiar and safe because of the people around me and impressive, courageous artists, but I also know that I have developed a connection with music that gives me complete certainty: No matter what happens, no matter how desperate I am, no matter how alone... I ALWAYS have the music. And that's a great feeling of safety!!!

That's why I take my guitar and my sheet music with me wherever I go for a longer period of time...even if I might not touch them once during that time, I need to feel that they are there if I would urgently need them. For my inner security feeling.

Thus, in my memories, music has politicized me and is strongly linked to images of safety and being connected. Music has always given mespace for emotions and pain, it was and often is a refuge to escape reality. Nevertheless, for me music also always means new beginnings, new strength, new glimmers of hope, empowerment, selfconfidence, and love.

In the context of our struggles for peace, for me, music is therefore a medium for processing the many overwhelming and cruel acts of violence, for touching and being touched, for forgetting and never forgetting, for feeling, healing, and creating hope, for meeting, understanding, empathizing and setting out together, for dreaming and fighting on...again and again. At this point, I would like to emphasize once again that I myself have the incredible privilege of being able to live in safety and that I don't know how I would feel about everything I have written here if I found myself in a different life situation, in a different place, in a different body. But maybe some people feel the same way... that in the end, music gives us confidence again: even if we have nothing left, we still have music.

Was macht mich sicher

***Mariana Lechterbeck**, Deutschland, Co-Vorsitzende der Internationalen Frauenliga für Frieden und Freiheit, 2024*

Vieles hängt damit zusammen, wie ich aufgewachsen bin. Sicher. Behütet. In vielerlei Hinsicht unglaublich privilegiert. Und mit viel Musik. Musik fühlt sich nach zuhause an. Ein Ort, der besonders wegen der lieben Menschen um mich rum, sicher ist. Ich erinnere mich an wunderschöne Jazz-Klänge morgens am Frühstückstisch.

Ich erinnere mich an antifaschistische und über häusliche Gewalt aufklärende Songs von den „Ärzten", an das „Kinderlied" von Joy Denelane, das meine Mama so oft für mich sang und ihr Lieblingslied von Joy „Wem gehört die Welt"…über Rassismus und Sexismus und über die Möglichkeit, die Welt noch verändern zu können. Ich erinnere mich an die großartige, laute und selbstbewusste Stimme meiner Mama (die natürlich zu jedem Anlass aus allen anderen Stimmen hervorstach und mir mit 14 unglaublich peinlich war hihi), aber auch daran, dass wir in schweren Zeiten oft zusammen zu Musik geweint haben. Ich denke an viele Autofahrten mit meinem Papa, auf denen wir mit Musik gemeinsam geträumt haben. Ich denke an herbstliche Nachmittage, an denen die sanften Klavierklänge meines Papas mich in das Wohnzimmer lockten, und ich einfach zuhören konnte. Ich denke an spontane Jam-Sessions mit der ganzen Familie, an Chorworkshops und meine kleinen Geschwister, die schon so jung von Musik fasziniert und begeistert waren, an die Frau meines Papas, die immer, selbst auf der Toilette, vor sich hinsingt und mein Papa, der viele selbstgereimte groovige Quatschlieder am Morgen summt, um uns allen einen guten Start in den Tag zu bereiten. Ich erinnere mich als kleines Kind so manches Mal auf Bänken neben lauten Musikboxen in Kneipen eingeschlafen zu sein, weil mein Papa einen Auftritt hatte, ich habe unendlich viele Bilder meines Papas an Keyboards und versunken im Rausch der Musik vor meinem Auge. Und dann denke ich natürlich ganz viel daran, wie ich Musik mache. Wie oft ich weinend am Klavier saß und mich selbst erst mit lauten und wütenden Hämmer-Akkorden austobte und dann ganz weichen melancholischen Klängen wieder beruhigte. Sich selbst in den Klängen der Musik, die man macht, zu verlieren, ist ein wunderschönes, faszinierendes, sicheres Gefühl. Ich weiß, dass Musik sich ganz viel wegen Menschen und mich rum und beeindruckenden mutigen Künstler*innen so vertraut und sicher anfühlt, aber ich weiß auch, dass ich dadurch eine Verbundenheit mit der Musik entwickelt habe, die mir die vollkommende Gewissheit gibt: Egal, was passiert, egal, wie verzweifelt ich bin, egal, wie alleine… ich habe IMMER die Musik. Und das, das ist ein großartiges Gefühl von Sicherheit!!! Deshalb nehme ich auch, egal, wo ich mich etwas länger aufhalte, meine Gitarre und meine Noten mit… auch wenn ich sie vielleicht in diesem Zeitraum kein einziges Mal berühre, brauche ich das Gefühl, dass sie da sind, wenn es dringend nötig wäre. Für meine Sicherheit.

In meinen Erinnerungen also hat mich Musik politisiert und ist stark an Bilder der Geborgenheit und des Verbunden-seins geknüpft. Musik hat mir schon immer Raum für Emotionen und Schmerz geschenkt, war und ist oftmals ein Zufluchtsort, um der Realität zu entkommen. Dennoch bedeutet Musik für mich auch immer Aufbruch, neue Kraft, neue Hoffnungsschimmer, Empowerment, Selbstvertrauen, Liebe.

Im Kontext unserer Kämpfe für den Frieden ist Musik für mich darum ein Medium zur Verarbeitung der vielen überfordernden und grausamen Gewalt, zum Berühren und Berührt-werden, zum Vergessen und gleichzeitig Niemals-Vergessen, zum Spüren, Heilen und Hoffnung-schöpfen, zum Begegnen, Begreifen, Mitfühlen und zum gemeinsamen Aufbrechen, zum Träumen und Weiterkämpfen…immer und immer wieder. An dieser Stelle möchte ich noch einmal betonen, dass ich selbst das unglaublich große Privileg habe, in Sicherheit leben zu können und dass ich nicht weiß, wie ich über all das hier Geschriebene denken würde, würde ich mich in einer anderen Lebenssituation, an einem anderen Ort, in einem anderen Körper wiederfinden. Aber vielleicht geht es der einen oder anderen Person ähnlich… dass am Ende auch hier Musik wieder die Zuversicht schenkt: Selbst wenn uns nichts mehr bleibt, dann bleibt uns doch noch und immer die Musik.

What Makes Me Feel Safe

Kathrin Winkler, *Canada*

Member of Nova Scotia Voice of Women for Peace, grandmother of 8 grand children, still enjoying life, using her energy to resist the war industry

Leaves even in their wild differences share a destiny to be rocked by the winds, stretch toward the sun and drift to the earth when the time comes. The power of their tenacious resistance helps me, the muddled old human grandmother, feel secure. I choose the freedom of the leaves as they twirl beyond human limitation that is trapped in the mechanized cruelty of endless warfare.

I acknowledge that we are in Mi'kma'ki, the ancestral and unceded territory of the Mi'kmaq People. This territory is covered by the "Treaties of Peace and Friendship" which Mi'kmaq and Wolastoqiyik (Maliseet) Peoples first signed with the British Crown in 1725. The treaties did not deal with surrender of lands and resources but in fact recognized Mi'kmaq and Wolastoqiyik (Maliseet) title and established the rules for what was to be an ongoing relationship between nations.

As descendants of Africans stolen from their homeland of Africa, Black Nova Scotians are owed reparations for centuries of inter-generational trauma from anti-Black racism rooted in chattel slavery, and for the systemic denial of opportunities to create wealth. Both continue to the present day.

White people benefit from these wrongs and as such have a responsibility to do their part to right these wrongs. We all will be stronger. Be brave.

What Makes Me Feel Safe

***Amani Aruri**, Palestinian human rights activist to advance economic well-being, social justice, human rights and Peace and Security Agendas in Palestine and the MENA region.*

For the moment my safety can just come from a cease-fire! Stop the bombing – we are human beings, we want to survive!

Our life is nevertheless not just about immediate survival. It is about occupation and oppression, continuous attacks on our lives, our land, our hopes and rights by a militarised state with extraordinary power. Every day on my way to work, I must pass through Israeli checkpoints. As a young woman and mother, I feel particularly vulnerable to abuse and humiliation by Israeli soldiers. It is difficult to describe the fear you experience when faced with an armed stranger whose only purpose is to oppress and intimidate you. More distressing was the powerlessness I felt as I was trying to protect my children.

Our struggle is also about societal norms, the underrepresentation of women in (political) spaces, lack of gender equality which proposes another layer of difficulties. In my society, young women are expected to bear the lion's share of the responsibility for child-rearing and housework with minimal participation from their father. Additionally, in case of a divorce, young women receive support neither from society nor from the state but instead suffer from discriminatory laws that favor men when it comes to alimony, custody, and other issues.

Raising our voices for Palestine is a universal fight for justice and resistance. We are not just victims! Currently, women's participation at the decision-making level does not exceed 1 percent, with no representation of young women. Women are excluded from participation in peace process negotiations and in talks to end the internal Palestinian division. You don't see a Palestinian women in negotiation or reconciliation tables – it was already in Camp David that women's voices were absent. This continues. We as Palestinian women have a different approach to the conflict - to make an end achievable. Palestinian women bring uniq inside especially regarding the humanitarian crisis.

Two years ago, I was nominated for the post of mayor in my area's municipality, but due to social and political pressures – mainly because I am a young woman – I was forced to withdraw from the elections. This experience, however, motivated me to work with other young people and establish a local youth council in my area that works parallel to the municipality.

I am born under the Intifada. I have developped skills, capacities and connections in the fields of social transformation, community activism, human rights, peace and security, advocacy, national dialogue and peace mediation to advance gender equality, economic wellbeing, social justice and human rights agendas at the national, regional and global levels. We young women can be powerful agents of social change. We have both the desire and the capacity to transform Palestinian social and political structures and are looking for opportunities to do so.

I am working with institutions, public and private foundations – so for me it is clear that peace building is only acceptable with the respect of human rights for all. But I feel silenced, I suffer from the restrictions of my freedom of expression to express my suffering. I feel censored by social media platforms, blacklisted by political decision makers also in my country, because I am very vocal since the beginning of the war in Gaza to explain the terrible reality on the ground.

Part of my reality is that if my children go to school in the morning, I have to control all the conditions, if the road is blocked, if they can make it, sometimes they may be attacked by settlers, their lives are on a daily basis under attack and they experience all kinds of intimidations.

We women – are extremely vulnerable regarding our sexual and reproductive rights. With the destruction of the health system, hospitals destroyed or severly damaged, no safe spaces and shelters, complications with maternity, as pregant women and mothers. Also sexual exploitation is an issue, sexual violence is absolutely overshadowed in this war in order not to be shown to the world.

We Palestinian women are not entitled to carry all the burden on our shoulders, we feel tired, feel hopless, always into conflict, intimidations, war.

I refuse to be silenced – I wanted to speak about the reality on the ground where our basic rights are continuously denied. We need solidarity. War doesn't have a feminin aspect, it kills everyones' hopes and aspiration to focus just on daily lifes, we are inspired for life and always think about the future despite patriarchy and occupation. We show our resistence and creativity in all aspects of life.

In addition, the problem is bigger: with the lack of access to clean water and healthy food.

We need and desserve solidarity! We act upon the main pillar of WPS agenda and the YPS agenda: on protection, participation and prevention with a major focus on women under occupation and locally

What Makes Me Feel Safe

***Afaf AlNajjar**, 22 year old Palestinian woman, citizen journalist, writer, marketing manager, a daughter, and sister.*

The Burden I Carry

I left behind a sky on fire,
But the flames still burn within my chest.
How do I live while they remain,
Trapped beneath the endless rain
Of bombs that tear through every rest?

Each night I fear the silence more,
A call unanswered – what will come next?
My parents linger on that shore,
While I walk free, but never blessed.
The weight of guilt, a constant guest.

What if I falter, what if I fall,
And all I've promised slips away?
How do I stand, how do I stay,
When every breath feels not my own,
And exile leaves me so alone?

Life here is waiting, nothing more –
A pause that stretches through the night.
The fear, the guilt, they wage their war,
While I survive but lose the fight.

I want to return, but skies still burn,
And will there be a home to see?
The road ahead feels sharp and steep –
I wake, I ache, I barely sleep –
My heart is there, but where is me?

What Makes Me Feel Safe

Shirin Jurdi, *Lebanon. Based on Interviews by Heidi Meinzolt*

Having lived a childhood of protracted conflict, exile and return, Shirine grew up with a belief that constant and continuing work towards peace, social cohesion and equality should be maintained. In 2003, Shirin joined WILPF-Lebanon. She works in research and training on issues pertaining to WPS agenda, women substantive and representative participation, conflict resolution, transitional justice and on R2P with a strong commitment from local to global and back. She is a member of GGPAC, in the steering committee of the Arab Feminist Network on WPS agenda and local councillor.

Nothing makes me feel safe anymore

I cannot sleep, we are in continuous alert, my sister calls me every hour, to be sure that we are still alive and safe when she sees again and again bombs and drones attacking our houses, killing people in the street, destroying schools and hospitals, causing thousands of displacements – people who have to leave their homes a second/third time – often not knowing anymore where to go and how to survive with all these losses.

No words can explain the pain! My mother doesn't stop crying and closes herselve in her appartment – re-traumatised by what she went through in her life. Nevertheless, fear and panic don't stop me trying everything to support people, to organise women from my environment, to protect girls from GBV. We can cry later! **My only safety is to be resilient myselve in the sense of resistence and the support of friends.**

The actual war from Israel is not just touching Hisbollah. It is causing an enormous amount of „civilian casualties". This war is just one episode in a long and tragic history of Lebanon. People will never get used to war, they continuosly struggle for peace and justice. We, Lebanese women clearly speak out about the war crimes and genocide going on in Gaza – we don't want to be a 2nd Gaza.

We need international solidarity to raise our voices, we need you to be our loudspeakers!

Where should our safety come from?

We are tired of all the desasters. The absence of a state order without forming institutions at the grassroots level, the vicious circle of religious and political bodies that have formed a religious-political confessional state in a religiously, culturally and politically very diverse country. There is no unified national identity. Lebanon is governed by six Muslim groups (Shi'a, Sunni, Druze, Isma'ili, Alawite or Nusayri), and 12 Christian sects (Maronite Catholic, Greek Orthodox, Melkite Catholic, Armenian Orthodox, Syrian Catholic, Armenian Catholic, Syrian Orthodox, Roman Catholic, Chaldean, Assyrian, Copt, Protestant). This religious-political alliance divides parliamentary seats, government, civil service and institutional offices among themselves in proportion to the religious population shares.

The 'October Revolution' of 2019 – triggered by new taxes on gas, tobacco and $6 on VoIP services such as WhatsApp – brought hundreds of thousands onto the streets calling for justice and demanding that corrupt politicians relinquish power. For almost 300 days, the protests plunged Lebanon into a severe socio-political crisis.

'The unfair political and confessional system leads politicians to divide offices among themselves again and again. In doing so, they deprive a large majority of the population of their rights.' While democracy in Lebanon actually allows room for free expression of disrespect, Jurdi says 'each faction only represents the interests of its own political and religious leaders. The survival of each group is based on a social structure that only serves its own clientele due to a corrupt system.'

Warlords who have mutated into politicians call the shots in their respective groups and the state serves as a kind of cover organisation for them. Over the past 30 years, the international community and the World Bank have funded Lebanon's post-civil war reconstruction efforts without any accountability during the transition.

The seeds of the October Revolution

'How can old warmongers and militia leaders now claim leadership roles? Those who stand for war cannot create peace. The now collapsing economic system, built purely on corruption and nepotism, distributed jobs, defined who could benefit from the education system, healthcare and hospitalisation, who had access to services and hygiene measures.

Throughout 2019, the motto for coexistence, alayesh moshtarak, united communities across socio-economic and religious divides - while politicians want the country divided to better control it. Lebanon's political decisions – backed by America, Iran and Saudi Arabia – have obviously always benefited one 'sect' and never the country as a whole. Lebanon's slight upturn in tourism has been thwarted by regular Israeli attacks across the southern border.

The hypocrisy of denying and not analysing all this has led to the collapse of all communities around us. Nothing is working anymore, except people's willingness to help. We help each other with only two hours of electricity a day because petrol is 'disappearing'. The energy minister is taking us for fools. It is annoying that while the Lebanese are starving, the banks are no longer handing out cash and political parties are still only catering for their own clientele. Actually we cannot even get our own money – and it is extremely difficult to receive money from abroad.

No safety – the explosion

In 2020, August 4th the explosion at the Beirut port brought back very concretely the lack of safety: „What we lived through is like watching a movie." For the last six years, the Council of Ministers, security sector and judicial authorities, aware of the dangerous chemicals stored at the port, took no preemptive measures to prevent a catastrophic accident in the densely populated capital city with over one million population. The 2,750 tons of ammonium nitrate containing 43.7 percent nitrogen is in violation of the law permitting only 11 percent–and if the government had a prioritized memo on the product's dangers, why didn't anyone take action? The pictures oft he explosion show like an atomic mushroom cloud and we thought this is the end! The first aid, fire-workers killed, hundreds dead, thousands insured, infrastructure and entreprises destroyed, hospitals evacuated, about 300.000 homeless, a follow up of escalating violence. Deep sorrow, great anger and again a terrible feeling of unsafety, ignorance, helplessness – confronted with blowing up violence, intransparency, total lack of accountability.

A minimum safety is needed for our dream of peace

We care about the most vulnerable, the many displaced persons, the lack of food, water, beds and shelters, specific sanitary needs of the women, reproductive health, medication, pain killers

We care about threats of gender-based violence, contribute to a feminist awarness in our society where patriarchal narratives are returning

We talk to institutions and the administration, (international) organisations, to women mediators network to be included in the process

We plead for immediate cease-fire, stop of weapons transfers to Israel, accountability and the de-construction of the values of deterrence for conflict prevention and de-militarisation.

We ask to take serious the protection pillar of WPS Agenda and the respective NAPs – where we see a tremendous deficit regarding women under pro-longed occupation. We need protection in the spirit of a real R2P (Responsibility to protect)

We appeal to UN, UN ambassadors in each country, to diplomats to stop genocide, to restrain from weapons delivery tot he agressors, to push for immediate cease-fires!

We raise our voices to tell the truth on the ground.

We need a critical mass to make a change! Please help us make it happen!

What Makes Me Feel Safe

***Nasrin Bijanyar**, Iranian woman living since many years in Abano Terme, Italy. Nasrin arrived in Italy directly after the fall of the Shah whom she opposed and the installation of Khomeini. Nasrin is a doctor and is continuously struggling for the rights of Iranian women together with the Italian diaspora. Interview by **Annalisa Milani**, Treviso, member of WILPF Italy and the CSP network.*

Security for me is being away from all situations that lead me to pain to risks and undesirable situations.

I left my country 46 years ago because I risked going to prison just for participating in demonstrations against the Shah of Iran. I came to Italy to be able to continue studying but the problems were not over.The revolution happened and Iran changed its appearance, religious fundamentalists arrived and took the country in the wrong direction.

My family thinks differently from them and so they become victims of extreme violence by the regime. My 23-year-old brother was killed by Passdaran because he did not accept their barbaric rules against women.

My sister was hanged after seven years in the medieval prison of the Iranian totalitarian regime. She is arrested and taken to prison while she was five months pregnant. She lost her baby under savage torture in the prison cells of Evin. And in the following years she also loses almost 80 per cent of her eyesight and so spends four years in total isolation and then in a three-minute trial without the right to a lawyer she is asked to cooperate with them to betray other opponents – and when she replies that 'my dignity is not for sale' she signs her death sentence at the age of 30.

What is security in a country that you are not sure you will see the dawn of the next day because you only think different from them, that there are no laws to protect a minimum of living without fear of being beaten to death by the husband, father, brother ...

In Iran, the Islamic penal code stipulates that anyone who commits a crime to defend someone else's life or reputation or chastity or honour should not be punished. but unfortunately, the application of this article is open to interpretation and manipulation, and this is how many Iranian women end up being sentenced to death despite having acted in self-defence.

There are many women in prison on death row for admitting to murder. They are very young and also mature. Iran ranks second after China in the world ranking of executioner countries, i.e. by the number of executions carried out per year.

After the killing of my brother and the arrest of my sister, my father is also arrested and ends up in prison without a trial and several times they simulated the execution scene to frighten him he had two heart attacks in the course of these simulations.

Again the passdarans return to my house and this time they arrest my other sister with her newborn baby and take her to prison, trials do not exist.

My desperate mother goes around asking for justice but in this country there is nothing just while my other sister suffers mistreatment for seven years in prison other family members suffer violence.

Zahra Bijanyar was hanged on a hot summer's day and after months of no news of her, the family was notified of the cruel side of the regime and also to go and get her bag of belongings. Her body is not there! It is not known where and how she was buried only we are told there is no right to any ceremony, the family's grief must be silenced. But my mum can't be quiet. She speaks where she goes. She speaks of the violence she has suffered, of the barbarities her family has had to endure.

There is Amnesty International in Teheran! She goes to talk to them and brings her family's story and the injustice she goes through in Iran, she vents her anger! When she comes down from the building where Amnesty International's delegation was, down in the street there are passdarans waiting for her.

„So you went to talk to the foreigners, we warned you not to do these things! Now you sign these documents that your children died of natural causes in your home! You refuse and keep saying that it was you who killed them." „I will not sign!" she said. And they answer: „ok now let's go and arrest your last daughter" (widowed at 24 with two small children). At this point my mother gives up and signs the damn document.

Amir Bijanyar an open and nice young man who and above all did not accept injustice, he was the first to be tortured with 70 whip lashes in the IRA for defending children who did not want to wear the obligatory veil. He was present at various demonstrations. He was active in taking the defence of the innocent, within a short time he was recognised and wanted! He escaped and took refuge in a house far from his parents' home, prepared the documents to escape from Iran. The very day he was to leave, at dawn the Passdaran attack his house and destroy it, razing it to the ground! All that remains of him is the motorbike parked nearby ...

Cosa è sicurezza per me

***Nasrin Bijayar**, donna iraniana che vive da molti anni ad Abano Terme. Nasrin è arrivata in Italia subito dopo la caduta dello Scià a cui si opponeva e l'insediamento di Khomeini. Nasrin è medico e lotta continuamente per i diritti delle donne iraniane insieme alla diaspora italiana. L'intervista è stata realizzata da **Annalisa Milani** / WILPF Italia e parte della rete CSP, residente a Treviso.*

La sicurezza per me è essere lontana a tutte le situazioni che mi porta a dolore ai rischi e alle situazioni indesiderabili.

Io ho lasciato il mio paese ancora 46 anni fa perché rischiavo di finire in prigione solo per aver partecipato alle manifestazioni contro lo Scià dell'Iran.

Vengo in Italia per poter continuare a studiare ma i problemi non sono finiti. accade la rivoluzione e l'iran cambia l'aspetto, arrivano i fondamentalisti religiosi che portano il paese in direzione sbagliata.

La mia famiglia pensa diversamente da loro e così diventano vittime di violenza estrema da parte del regime.

Mio fratello di 23 anni viene ucciso da parte di Passdaran perché non accettava le loro regole barbariche contro le donne.

Mia sorella viene impiccata dopo sette anni di carcere medioevale del regime totalitario iraniano. Lei viene arrestata e portata in prigione mentre era al quinto mese di gravidanza. perde il suo bimbo sotto la tortura selvaggia nelle celle di carcere di evin. E negli anni successivi perde anche la vista quasi 80% e così passa quattro anni in isolamento totale e poi in un processo di 3 minuti senza poter avere diritto di un avvocato le viene chiesto di collaborare con loro e andare in giro per riconoscere altri oppositori e quando lei risponde che „la mia dignità non è in vendita" firma la sua condanna a morte a età di 30 anni.

Cos'è la sicurezza in un paese che non sei sicuro di vedere l'alba del giorno dopo perché solo Pensi diverso da loro,che non ci sono le leggi che tutelino un minimo di vivere senza paura di essere picchiata a morte dal marito padre fratello ...

In Iran il codice penale islamico prevede che chiunque commetta un crimine per difendersi la vita di qualcun altro o reputazione o la castità oppure l'onore, non dovrebbe essere punito. ma purtroppo l'applicazione di questo articolo è suscettibile di interpretazione e manipolazione è così che molte donne iraniane finiscono per essere condannate a morte pur avendo agito per legittima difesa.

Ci sono tante donne in carcere in braccio della morte per aver ammesso un omicidio. sono giovanissime e anche in età matura. Iran e al secondo posto dopo la Cina nella graduatoria mondiale dei paesi boia cioè per numeri di esecuzioni che viene effettuato all'anno.

Dopo uccisione di mio fratello e arresto di mia sorella, viene arrestato anche mio padre finisce in carcere senza un processo e più volte hanno simulato la scena di esecuzione per spaventarlo lui in percorso di queste simulazioni ha fatto ben due infarti.

Di nuovo i passdaran tornano a casa mia e questa volta arrestano l'altra mia sorella con la sua bimba neonata e la portano in prigione, i processi non esistono.

Mia mamma disperata va in giro a chiedere la giustizia ma in questo paese di giusto non c'è niente mentre l'altra mia sorella subisce maltrattamenti per sette anni in carcere altri membri della famiglia subiscono violenza.

Zahra Bijanyar in un giorno caldo di estate viene impiccata e dopo mesi di assenza di notizie di lei, la famiglia viene avvisata del lato crudele del regime e anche per andare a prendere la sua borsa di effetti personali. La sua salma non c'è! Non si sa dove e come è stata seppellita solo ci dicono non avete il diritto di nessuna cerimonia „il dolore della famiglia deve essere azzittita. Però mia mamma non sa essere zitta. Lei parla dove va. Parla della violenza subita delle barbarie che la sua famiglia ha dovuto sopportare.

C'è Amnesty International a Teheran! Lei parte, va a parlare con loro e porta con sé la storia della sua famiglia e l'ingiustizia che percorre in Iran, si sfoga! Quando scende dal palazzo dove c'era la delega di Amnesty International giù in strada ci sono i passdaran che la aspettano

„Allora sei andata a parlare con gli stranieri, ti avevamo avvisato di non fare queste cose! Ora tu firmi questi documenti che i tuoi figli sono morti per le cause naturali a casa tua!" Lei rifiuta e continua a dire che siete stati voi a ucciderli e io non firmerò! E loro rispondono: „va bene ora andiamo ad arrestare l'ultima tua figlia" (vedova a 24 anni con due bimbi piccoli). A questo punto mia madre cede e firma quel maledetto documento.

Amir Bijanyar un ragazzo curioso gentile e bravo e soprattutto non accettava l'ingiustizia, lui è stato il primo ad essere torturato a 70 colpi di fruste in IRA per difendere i ragazzini che non volevano portare il velo obbligatorio. Lui era presente in vari manifestazioni Era attivo a prendere la difesa dei innocenti in giro di poco tempo viene riconosciuto e ricercato! Lui scappa e si rifugia in una casa lontano da casa dei genitori, prepara i documenti per scappare dall'iran. Il giorno stesso che doveva partire, all'alba i passdaran attaccano la casa sua e la distruggono, raso al solo! Da lui resta solo la moto parcheggiato là vicino ...

What Makes Me Feel Safe

Arwa Elabd, *Egypt, Austria*

*„Damit junge Menschen lesen, brauchen sie Literatur, die sie anspricht. Diese bietet ihnen Arwa Elabd in ihrer Buchhandlung." **

As a Muslim woman, safety for me is multi-faceted. I find comfort and security within my own community, where I am embraced without needing to explain myself, and where I am accepted for who I truly am. It's a space where I can feel at ease, knowing that I am understood and valued.

I feel safe when I am surrounded by people who bring out the best in me, who inspire and uplift me. Those who genuinely believe in my potential, and where I, too, have the chance to help others shine – supporting them with the knowledge I've gained. There is something truly special about the relationships that allow for mutual growth and encouragement.

My local mosque has always been a sanctuary, a place I have known since childhood. The very sight of it, or even the thought, makes my heart open and fill with light. It's a space where everyone is welcome, where I've always felt a sense of belonging, and where I can reconnect with my faith and find inner peace.

Islam, for me, is a constant source of protection and comfort, no matter where I am in the world. In every mosque I've visited, whether in a bustling city or a quiet village, there is an undeniable feeling of unity. Even if we do not speak the same language, we share the same love for Allah, and that bond is unbreakable. It's a beautiful reminder that wherever I go, I am not alone.

I also find safety in the presence of my family and friends. The warmth of their love is a reminder that I am cherished and supported. And then, there's my bookstore – a place where I've poured my heart and soul. It's not just a business, but a space for connection, learning, and growth. Here, I feel grounded, surrounded by the stories of others, and sharing my own journey through the books I choose to showcase.

These places and relationships form a tapestry of security that wraps around me, allowing me to navigate the world with confidence and peace.

* *Ute Brühl, Bibliobox, Kurier, Austria, 19.01.2024*

What Makes Me Feel Safe

***Aina Shormanbayeva**, Kazakhstan, co-founder and head of International Legal Initiative (ILI), independent human rights organization. She was born in a family whose history has been closely related to the history of Kazakh land for at least 500 years.*

My home and family are the source of peace and safety for me. I grew up in an atmosphere of commitment to knowledge, education, the leading role of women in the development of their families and society. The source of danger has always been the state. I was born during the Soviet Union, where the system did not allow freedom and independence of the individual. However, it was in the family of descendants of people repressed by the Soviet system that I absorbed the spirit of freedom and independence.

There were situations when I risked my life to protect human rights, risked the peace and safety of my family to protect the public interest. But my family has always been and she is my support, in the family I find strength and power.

In turn, so that not only my family, but also other families in Kazakhstan feel safe and protected, I chose 22 years ago the path of a human rights defender. Then I did not know what human rights are. I did not know that instead of becoming a pianist, I would become a lawyer and defend the human rights of those who were not helped by the state. Since then, thousands of people have been able to protect their rights with our help and this makes my world safer. I move forward on my path every day and every small or significant victory or achievement gives strength, confidence and a sense of security to those we help. I remember the story of a Kazakh woman from East Turkestan (Xinjiang), teacher of Kazakh school. She was separated from her family for 4 years, Chinese authorities didn't allow her to move to Kazakhstan and unite with her husband and son. She suffered alone in repressive atmosphere while her husband went to court of Kazakhstan with our help to save his family. We could help this woman, she was allowed to move to Kazakhstan and unite with her family. Then we helped her to get Kazakhstani citizenship, provided medical and psychological assistance and now she is well and happy with her family. After her returning to the family we met in our office and she cried and said that there are the people in the world who care her, helping and protecting her. It was so touching. This is not the only example of the results of our work to make the world more safe for women from East Turkestan, where indigenous people – ethnic Kazakhs, Uyghurs, Uzbeks, Kyrgyzs and other Turk people suffering crime against humanity. We helped at least 1000 women from this region in the last 7 years. Among them there are the members of separated families, victims of torture from concentration camps, whom we helped to be released and move to Kazakhstan, to more safe place for them and their families. In addition, I'm providing free legal assistance to 500 women from rural areas through WhatsApp groups. They have no access to free legal assistance and justice and these every days consultations are the only way to resolve their problems. These women have families and our help is the help to the whole family.

I am happy that my life has turned out this way. I have many friends, colleagues, like-minded people, I am not alone on my path. When the people supporting you are shoulder to shoulder close to you, you feel safe. These people become your large family. Together, step by step, we change the world for the better where we are. It is a difficult path, but I like this journey.

Айна Шорманбаева*, Халықаралық Құқықтық Бастаманың (ILI) тәуелсіз құқық қорғау ұйымының құрылтайшысы және жетекшісі. Мен Қазақ Елінің кем дегенде 500 жылдық тарихына тығыз байланысы бар отбасында дүниеге келдім.*

Өз үйім мен отбасым мен үшін тыныштық пен қауіпсіздіктің қайнар көзі. Менің отбасымда білім алу, жан-жақты даму, әйелдердің отбасыда да, қоғамда да алда жүретін орны бар деген көзқарас басым болды. Біз үшін қауіп әркез мемлекет тарапынан төнген. Мен Кеңес Одағы тұсында дүниеге келдім, бұл жүйеде жеке адамның еркіндігі мен тәуелсіздігіне жол берілмеді. Кеңестік жүйе репрессиясына ұшырағандардың ұрпақтары шаңырағында еркіндік пен тәуелсіздік рухын бойыма сіңірдім.

Адам құқығын қорғау үшін өмірімді қатерге тігіп, қоғамдық мүдденi қорғау үшін отбасымның тыныштығы мен қауіпсіздігіне қауіп төнген жағдайлар болды. Осындай кездерде де, әркез отбасым менің тірегім болып, маған күш-қуат береді.

Өз отбасым ғана емес, Қазақстанның басқа да отбасылары өздерін қауіпсіз және қорғалуда екенін сезіну үшін мен осыдан 22 жыл бұрын құқық қорғаушы жолын таңдадым. Ол кезде адам құқығы не екенін білмедім. Пианист болудың орнына заңгер болып, мемлекеттен көмек ала алмағандардың адам құқығын қорғайтынымды білген жоқпын. Содан бері мыңдаған адамдар біздің көмегіміз арқасында өз құқықтарын қорғай алды. Осының өзі жан-дүниеме қауіпсіздік әкелетіндей болады. Осы жолымнан таймай, күн сайын алға басып, әрбір кішігірім болса да, маңызды жеңіске жеткеніміз қорғауымыздағы адамдарға күш, сенімділік және қауіпсіздік сезімін сыйлайды.

Бір оқиға әлі есімде. Шығыс Түркістаннан (Шыңжаңнан) келген қазақ мектебінде сабақ берген мұғалім әйел 4 жыл бойы отбасынан бөлініп, Қытай билігі тарапынан қысымға түсіп, Қазақстандағы күйеуі мен баласына бара алмай, отбасымен қосылуына рұқсаты жоқ болды. Жолдасы біздің көмегімізбен Қазақстан биліктерніен көмек сұрап, арызданған кезде бұл әйел жападан-жалғыз қалып қойып, қатты күйзеліске түсті. Көмектің арқасында оған Қазақстанға көшіп, отбасымен қосылуға рұқсат етілді. Одан кейін Қазақстан азаматтығын алуға көмектестік, медициналық және психологиялық көмек көрсеттік, қазір оның жағдайы жақсы, отбасымен бақытты өмір сүруде. Ол отбасына оралғаннан кейін кеңсемізде кездестік, ол бұл әлемде оған қамқорлық жасайтын, көмектесетін және оны қорғайтын адамдар бар екен деп жылап айтты. Оның сөздері маған қатты әсер етті.

Бұл Шығыс Түркістандағы байырғы халықтар – этникалық қазақтар, ұйғырлар, өзбектер, қырғыздар және басқа да түркі халықтарға адамзатқа қарсы қылмыс жасалып жатқанда, әйелдер үшін әлемді қауіпсіз ету жөніндегі жұмыс нәтижесінің жалғыз мысалы емес. Соңғы 7 жылда осы аймақтағы кем дегенде 1000 әйелге көмектестік. Олардың арасында концлагерьлерде азаптау құрбандары болған, бөлінген отбасылар мүшелері бар, біз олардың босатылуына, Қазақстанға көшіп келуге, отбасыларына қосылуына көмектестік. Сонымен қатар, WhatsApp топтары арқылы ауылдық жерде тұратын 500-ге жуық әйелдерге ақысыз заңгерлік көмек көрсетіп жатырмыз. Олар сондай заңгерлік көмек пен әділеттілікке қол жеткізе алмайды және күнделікті кеңес алу арқасында мәселелерін шешуде. Осы әйелдердің де отбасылары бар, бір әйелге берілген көмек бүкіл отбасына көмек болады.

Өмірім осындай болғанына қуаныштымын. Менің достарым, әріптестерім, пікірлестерім көп, өз жолымда жалғыз емеспін. Сізді қолдайтын адамдар өзіңізге иық тіресе жақын болса, өзіңізді қауіпсіз сезінесіз. Олар үлкен отбасыңыз болады. Бірлесе отырып, әлемді жақсы жаққа өзгертеміз. Бұл оңай емес, бірақ өзіме осы саяхат ұнайды.

Turkmen version of „Kinder, Küche, Kirche" continues.

Tajigul Begmedova*, PHD professor and candidate of sciences, teacher at University for over 20 years. Due to persecution by the regime, she is a human rights activist. In 2003, she founded the human rights organisation called Turkmenistan Helsinki Foundation for Human Rights.*

The Turkmen authoritarian regime considers human rights defenders and activists „traitors to the Motherland". Because of this, for more than 20 years I have not been able to return to my homeland and do what I love with my family. I was not there for my parents when the regime persecuted and abused them. They were buried without me, and to this day I am unable to visit their graves and pay my respects. Similarly with my husband's sister a Radio Liberty journalist, who was killed by the regime in prison.

During the pandemic, Turkmen migrants rose up in Turkey, as some might call it the first protest movement. THF was one of the first to respond to this call from Turkmen migrants, helping them to assert their rights. For this, under pressure from the Turkmen regime, Ankara twice banned me from entering Turkey. The first time I managed to restore my right to freedom of movement through the courts. Last year, the Turkish authorities again have denied me an entry to Istanbul, thanks to the authoritarian regime of Turkmenistan.

22 years ago, after my husband and I left Turkmenistan, the authorities fabricated a criminal case against us for an incident that occurred in our absence. The authorities in Bulgaria, where we moved to after receiving a request from Turkmenistan, did not even bother to look into the matter, but for the sake of geopolitical interests tried to serve the Turkmen dictator. For this purpose, they started to persecute us in various ways, breaking the law. My husband and I were detained for 2 weeks, leaving our minor child alone in a foreign country. As a mother, I was very scared for my child, but no one responded to my worries. In our absence, my daughter was bitten by a dog on her way to school, but no one helped her. Moreover, she was terrorized at school, being called the daughter of criminals.

Then the Bulgarian police made a second, more insidious attempt to fulfill the Turkmen regime`s order. They decided to separate me from my family: one night the police came to our house and tried to illegally deport me to dictator Turkmenistan, although my documents were in order. Apparently, they hoped that my daughter and husband would voluntarily follow me.

We took Bulgarian authorities to court and the court of a European country recognised that Turkmen accusations were of political persecution. Turkmenistan did not dare to appeal this decision, knowing that everything was initially falsified by the Turkmen prosecutor office.

For more than 20 years I have been living and fighting against the struggle of Turkmens and for their rights as human beings, it is good that I am supported by my family. All my free time, experience and opportunities are aimed at helping my compatriots. Our relatives back home rely on us, as they have no opportunity to stand up for human rights, as Turkmenistan is one of the last places in the world in terms of restriction of rights and freedoms. But there are still people who on regular basis organise online harassment and harassment against me through Internet platforms. Note that most of them are men!

I am from a large family and my spouse has 10 brothers and sisters, we always lived modestly. I remember sometimes I didn`t even have 4 „kopeiki" (pence or cents) for the bus and had to walk long distances with heavy grocery bags.

Since childhood I have been very compassionate and at the same time I have a very high sense of justice. Because of this, I cannot stand aside when people are suffering, especially women and children. In the eastern country where I come from, a woman is given a place as in the famous German phrase: „Kinder, Küche, Kirche". In Turkmen realities, it is the husband, children, household, as well as the husband`s relatives. Social life/work remains in the last place. Moreover, it is believed that a woman by nature is not capable of anything more than „KKK".

To understand the level of attitude of Turkmen society towards Turkmen women, I will give you the simplest example from my life. Once, during a morning jog, a stranger threatened me: „Go back home! How can a Turkmen woman wear jogging pants and a T-shirt instead of a long dress! What are your parents thinking?" Another time, I went to the University in moccasins, but on the way several times young men made remarks to me that I was wearing „men`s" shoes, not heels! This was in the 80s. Unfortunately, the situation has not improved so far, especially in the periphery.

The foreign public was outraged by reports in recent years that Turkmen women are required by the authorities to wear national dresses, they are not allowed to drive a car, get makeup, manicures, dye their hair, walk in the city holding hands with their beloved boyfriend/husband, not to mention hugging, girls are tested for virginity in schools, and young girls may not be allowed to go abroad at the airport without a relative accompanying them. Women are afraid to complain to the police about domestic violence because of social stigma, as „you can`t take it out of the house". Harassment of Turkmen women by their bosses at work is perceived as normal. The authorities do not recognize the existence of these problems, deliberately presenting the propaganda of customs and traditions as a concern for gender equality.

For many decades, the problems of the Aral Sea have not been solved, for which hundreds of thousands of Turkmen women are suffering from various diseases, and the burning gas crater in Turkmenistan, called „the gates of hell"pollutes the planet. Instead of directing the achievements of mankind to such problems, mankind produces weapons to destroy itself, and in such countries as Turkmenistan the cult of personality is glorified not without connivance of the international community. Instead of developing intellect, dictatorship is imposed, as well as duplicity and corruption. And such concepts as democracy, liberalism, tolerance are so leveled out that they hide self-interest and cruelty.

I am also very concerned about what is happening in the world. Who could have thought that in the 21st century there would be military actions on the territory of Europe, because of which the world is seeing thousands and thousands human victims? There is so much aggression in the world, and all attempts to explain simple truths are met with ignorance, rudeness and impunity. Is this what we will leave to our children and grandchildren?

A whole century has passed, but the words of Mark Twain are still relevant: „The nation is divided into patriots and traitors, and no one is able to distinguish one from the other."

What Makes Me Feel Safe

Elena Erkingul, *Kirgisztan,*

human rights activist, environmental activist, parlamentarian

Women, taking into consideration their bravery in childbirth, can increase the world population, they can also change the world and protect it from environmental catastrophe, no more no less!

However, women's labor is often exploited by men who sideline them and appropriate the results of their labor!

I have experienced it as well. Politicians took advantage of my work, saying, „I did it," using my materials for their own purposes. They deceived people, became presidents, deputies!

I was born in the village, lived and studied there. I was raised by a not-so-literate war veteran and home front veteran. I used to read books to them when I was little.

I was born in the most beautiful place, on the shore of a lake, in the foothills, near glaciers.

A transnational gold mining company came here and began to destroy this beauty. They destroyed the soil, destroyed glaciers, poisoned lakes, poisoned people, disabled children, which subsequently led to deaths, women were forced to have an abortion, they insulted them and made them cry!

I sat down and thought: if not me, then who else will protect people and the soil, who will protect the glaciers that provide us with clean water? In 1998, in order to protect our environment, I acted as a human rights activist protecting the rights of people affected by the cyanide accident caused by the Kumtor Operating Company. I was harassed, threats were made not only to me, but also to my brothers and sisters. My mother cried and said: „Give up this work of yours, they'll kill you for this work!" But I couldn't give up what I had started, because I had people behind me begging and hoping for me!

The company and the government did not listen to the demands of the people. Corrupt government leaders supported the company and trampled on the people.

But we were united, the people supported me. They tried to arrest me several times, but the people did not give them this opportunity. Both in summer and cold winter, we stood firm in blocking the company's road. As a result, the company had to pay people compensation for lost profits on crops in the amount of $ 4.5 million.

For 15 years, I have sued the company in the courts, fought for justice and recovered moral damages from the company in favor of 17 victims!

Most importantly, I forced the company, which easily took the corrupt local government into its hands, to admit its guilt, finally bowing its head to the population. I forced the government, rotten with wealth, to surrender the gold mining company, which easily bribed it.

I proved that not everything in the world is sold for gold!

I came to the parliament, solved the problems of the people, joined the committee on environmental protection, created a state commission and developed a law on the protection of glaciers.

Glaciers are a source of clean water for people. Man cannot survive without clean water! The glaciers of Kyrgyzstan supply clean water to all countries of Central Asia. There is a risk of leaving millions of people without water hoping to get some gold.

I think that what I have done will help many women, because justice will prevail anyway!

Айымдар дуйно жузундогу адамзаатты кобойтуп, бала торогон эрдиктен башка аялдар дуйнону озгортуп жана дуйнону экологиялык катастрофадан сактай алат!

Бирок аялдардын эмгегин эркектр коп учурда колдонуп аларды экинчи оорунга койушат озулору эмгекти ыйарып алышат!

Менин практикамда да ошондой болду менин жасаган иштеримди саясатчылар кондонушту «мен жасадым» деп менин материалдарымды озулорунун ишине колдонуп элди алдашты ошону менен президент депутат болушту!

мен айыл жергесинде торолуп айылда окуп чонойгом мени карган сабатсыз согуштун ветераны жана тылдын арадагери багып чонойткон. Мен кичинемде аларга китеп окуп берчумун

Мен эн кооз жерде торолгом колдун жээгинде тоонун алдында ан монгунун жанында

Ошол кооздукту транснационалдык алтын казган компания келип буза башташты жерди томкоруп монгуну талкалап колду уулантып элди уулантып инвалид кылып балдарды олумго алып келип аялдардын бойунан алдыртып кордоп ыйлатты!

Отуруп ойлондум мен болбосом башка болбосо ким элди жерди коргойт таза сууну камсыз кылган монгуну ким коргойт! Экологиябызды сакташ учун 1998 жылы «Кумтор Оперейтинг Компаниясынын» куноосу менен цианиддик авриядан жабыркаган элдин укугун коргоо учун мен башымды сайып укук коргоочу болуп алдыга чыктым. Куугунтук болду мага эле эмес бир-туугандарыма чейин коркутушту. Апам ыйлады «таштачы ушул ишинди олтуруп кетет» деди бирок баштаган ишимди таштай алган жокмун анткени артымда жалдырап менден умут кылган эл турду!

Элдин унун талаптарыбызды компания да Окмот да уккан жок элди тооткон жок коррупцияга малынган окмот башчылар компанияны колдоду элди тебеледи. Бирок биз биримдикте турдук эл мени колдоду.

Бир канча жолу мени камаганга арекет кылышты бирок эл бербеди. Жайында суук кышта да биз жол тосуп компанияны жолун тосуп жудоттук акыры компания элге алынбай калган тушумдун компенцассиясын 4.5 миллион доллар толоп бергенге аргасыз болду.

15 жыл сотто компания менен соттошуп акыйкат учун курошуп 17 жабыркаган адамга моралдык чыгымды компаниядан ондуруп бердим! Эн негизгиси мен байлыка чиренген бийликти да оной сатып алган алтын казган компанияны чоголотуп багындырып айласыз башын жерге салып куноосун мойнуна алганга аргасыз кылдым.

Дуйнода баары эле алтынга акчага сатылбасын далилдедим!

What Makes Us Feel Safe

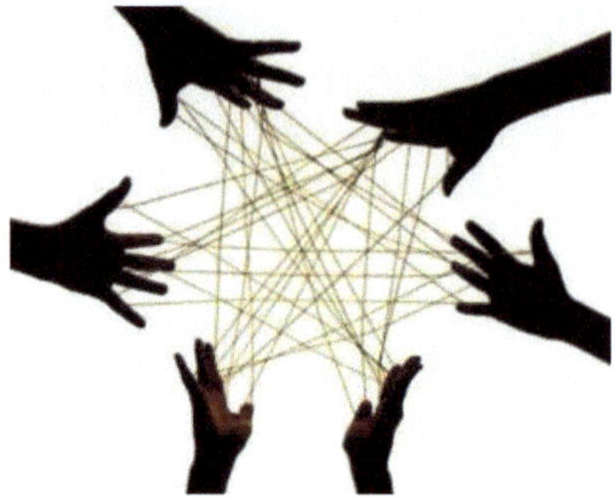

Teresa Lapis, *Italian lawyer, university lecturer, expert in peace-building on academic and grass-root level*

WHAT'S THE PROBLEM?

If the problem is to build a community that is about freedom, peace and women, we will have to share a sense of community and make it a singular, plural and shared manifesto on Chronospatiality.

CHRONOSPATIALITY

is a concept to reconcile planning and responsibility between energy needs and resource management: Responsibility is understood as taking charge of the prejudices to be dispelled. Planning is understood as action to escape from the traps of the anthropocene and directed towards transformation taking into account (new) feminist occasions. Planning is understood also in relation to a discontinuity that characterises a process of re-defining well-being between the good-having and the good-being.

COMMUNITY

is understood in a FEMINIST PERSPECTIVE where women denounce the need to speak the truth in order not to waste this crisis by opposing digital feudalism. If by security/safety we understand the guarantee of rights and the recognition of facts, then we are not afraid to express that „we are the witches" in, for example, denouncing the role of modern medicine in their repression of women.

Security then, means a guaranty or certainty and hope and not object of social control of what might be understood as dangerous.

VISIBILITY

if by visibility we understand the management and social internalisation of diversity, the problem is how to deal with the stigma that is present in all societies wherever moral rules come into play for the definition of identities. We need to ask ourselves what are the strategies for the defence or adaptation of stigmatised people and therefore what is the gap between social identity and feminist identity in a perspective between normality and deviance.

PERSPECTIVE

Our activism is no longer based strategically on pacifist feminists because our perspective is not to win a battle but to change the world, in an expectation of global justice based on solidarity, subsidiarity, conflict management: Criminal law and women's crimes could be approached from a social perspective by changing the current approach of the simple criminalisation of women, controlled by institutions: women are essentially victims in a scenario where women's power to create life is subject to control, excluding the proposal of 'family and domestic work = care', as a guarantee of the effectiveness of the social pact between the state and civil society. We need to construct a glocal system of social care/security, focusing on the position of women, feminists. Citizenship must be understood as a complex of rights guaranteed for the legally provided expectation that reconciles freedom and equality.

FROM GOOD TO HAVE TO GOOD TO BE

In a transnational perspective, the polical impact can be: crossing the boundaries of the welfare state of the common goods, towards a welfare state that expresses social rights with the practice of change and self-regulation that builds a society as a community. It opens up the discussion for subalternity studies with a specific focus on gender co-domain issues to reinvent politics and move from smart city to smart land.

CIVIL SOCIETY

We understand civil society by an enlarged state or an integrated state, where we identify a connection between politics, economics and civil society. WILPF's should be the promoter of the new concept of civil society of the millennium as a community not in reference to the pre-capitalist one but in the global perspective, for a Constitution of the Earth – based on effective equality, between elements of nature and those structured by human activity, referring to the paradigm of sustainable development understood as connected to the feminist approach of motherhood. This is to reconcile freedom and peace.

PROCESS

If by process we mean the road from Cairo to Beijing, in the context of women's rights and achievements in Beijing (for example), we verify the centrality of issues for health protection, violence against women, the effects of war, access to economic structures, power sharing and decision-making as mechanisms required to promote women's advancement and universal human rights.

The term „gender" has been commonly used and generally accepted until 2030. At this point, one should monitor the different ways of understanding equality and fairness or equality and dignity that still show deficits in their application and consideration as human rights.

The political difference highlights the possibility of writing the discussed and shared rules for the Constitution of the Earth that is based on the scrap of memory beyond violence and myth, prioritising the participation of the government in respect of the social structures in decision-making processes and public discourse.

HOW TO PROCEED

- Telling our stories
- Choosing objectives between criticality and benefits
- Participating in public debates with a welcoming and engaging presence - betweenlogbook and a dialogue, between knowledge and intergenerational dialogue
- Certain, transparent and shared debate with accessible documents and well-founded justifications
- Anti-hierarchical comunication forms, consistent with the mission and innovations
- Constructive criticism with equal time and space for all
- Verification of understanding and learning through democratic sharing
- Awareness raising of interdependence and political representation, consistent with feminist representation for peace and freedom
- Respecting an activist (no longer militant), constructive and non-strategic language to guarantee clarity in working progress in the continuous search for feedback.

What Makes Us Feel Safe?

Anki Wetterhall, *Operation 1325, Stockholm 2024*

Women have an important role to create and keep a sustainable peace. Therefore it is of great importance that women have knowledge of their human rights, get involved and, in different ways, take an active role in the peace process, both locally and internationally.

In 2000 the UN Security Council Resolution 1325 on Women, Peace and Security was adopted. Which was the first time that women's full participation in conflict management was established as a matter of international peace and security

Several Swedish women´s and peace organisations discussed together how to work to implement this important Resolution into reality. In 2003, the umbrella organisation Operation 1325, was founded. Operation 1325 works in Sweden and in partnership with peace- and women´s organisations around the world with the aim of implementing the UN´s Security Council´s Resolution 1325 on Women, Peace and Security

Through advocacy and training in Sweden and internationally, the organisation´s objective is to increase women´s influence at all levels of peace processes and in conflict resolutions. Operation 1325 advocates, informs, educates and creates platforms for debate and dialogue to influence decision makers, civil society and the general public with the aim of implementing the Resolution 1325. The Resolution 1325 should have an impact on all peace-keeping operations, development work as well as military and civilian operations everywhere.

Operation 1325 is also a part of the Swedish OSCE-network which works with the values of OSCE, Organisation for Security and Cooperation in Europe.

Operation 1325 works internationally to create partnership with women's and peace organisations from different parts of the world such as Palestine, Turkey and a lot of networks in Eastern Europe, Middle East and Northern Africa.

Through advocacy and training, in Sweden and internationally, the organisation's objective is to increase women's influence at all levels of peace processes and in conflict resolution.

Mediation network and training in Mediation

Although much progress has been made since the adoption of UN Security Council Resolution 1325, women are still excluded from processes such as peace talks and negotiations. Women as mediators are also underrepresented. Operation 1325 therefore works to train women mediators, build networks for active mediators, and strengthen women's participation in peace and security issues.

For example, together with the Palestinian Centre for Peace and Democracy (PCPD), we did the project „Women's Mediation School" in Palestine for mediation and networking. The project aimed to increase the power and agency of young women under 30 by supporting local women leaders, activists and women's organizations.

Advisory in multilateral networks

Operation 1325 plays an important role as an advisor to several multilateral networks. We have for example been member of NATO's Civil Society Advisory Panel on Women, Peace and Security. The group's purpose was to serve as a forum for dialogue and feedback from civil society to NATO on issues related to women, peace and security. Since March 2024 Sweden is a new member of NATO and we will of course continue the work to influence the organization through our government.

Education in equal pecebuilding

Since 2003, Operation 1325 has worked with training and workshops as a means of strengthening women's influence in peace processes. The training is aimed at civil society organisations around the world, personnel in peacekeeping operations, and other actors who work in conflict and post-conflict areas. Courses are tailored and based on the needs of the participants.

Project in Palestine

In Palestine, women live in a society characterised by patriarchal structures and norms that place women outside the public sphere and within the private sphere. Our work in Palestine provides women with tools to both change and strengthen women's rights and participation in decision-making and peace-building processes.

Operation 1325 has been working with women's organisations, locally as well as nationally, in Palestine, since the start of our organisations work. The projects focus on raising awareness of women's rights and women's role in peacebuilding, as well as empowering women to participate in peace processes.

In recent years, we have had many projects and partnerships in Palestine. In 2023, the MENA programme of the Operation 1325 communication project was launched with the aim of increasing women's participation in peace processes.

In recent years, we have had a lot of cooperation with our partners Palestinian Centre for Peace and Democracy (PCPD) and Palestinian Working Women Society (PWWSD).

Cooperation with our partners in Palestine goes back many years. Past and present projects have given us the opportunity and space for continuous communication and consultation.

In 2022, we implemented a project that brought together women from Yemen, Iraq and Sudan. The countries share a similar conflict status where women are excluded from the political process and, therefore, we saw an opportunity for interaction and impact.

The activities aimed to achieve visibility and give status to the women. Through capacity-building activities on relevant working methods for participating in peace processes and conflict management, women gain legitimacy and thus become visible as peace actors, which in turn leads to pressure for change towards decision-makers.

The activities were well designed to enable the creation of a forum, an egalitarian network, where women's own needs and wishes for increased knowledge determine the content and where knowledge can be shared and deepened in a trusting manner.

Similar projects as in Palestine, have been done also in Jemen.

In 2022, we implemented a project that brought together women from Yemen, Iraq and Sudan. The countries share a similar conflict status where women are excluded from the political process and, therefore, we saw an opportunity for interaction and impact.

The activities aimed to achieve visibility and give status to the women. Through capacity-building activities on relevant working methods for participating in peace processes and conflict management, women gain legitimacy and thus become visible as peace actors, which in turn leads to pressure for change towards decision-makers.

The activities were well designed to enable the creation of a forum, an egalitarian network, where women's own needs and wishes for increased knowledge determine the content and where knowledge can be shared and deepened in a trusting manner.

Conclusions

For women to feel more safe it is of utmost importance that they learn more about their human rights, to get organised locally, nationally or internationally, to learn how to influence the public, decision makers etc, In this article I have mentioned the work of the Swedish organisation 1325 and some of the projects we have delt with. Depending on the political situation in many countries, and also difficulties in Sweden to receive fundings we only work in Palestine at the moment. We still keep in contact with organisations in Sudan, Turkey and other countries and hope that we manage to continue our work soon.

Vad kan få kvinnor att känna sig trygga?

Anki Wetterhall, *Stockholm, Operation 1325*

Kvinnor har en viktig roll när det gäller att skapa och behålla en hållbar fred. Därför är det ytterst viktigt att kvinnor skaffar sig kunskap om sina grundläggande mänskliga rättigheter, engagerar sig och, på olika sätt, tar en aktiv roll i fredsprocessen såväl på lokal som internationell nivå.

Från Resolution till verksamhet

År 2000 antog FN:s säkerhetsrådsresolution 1325 om kvinnor, fred och säkerhet vilket var första gången som kvinnors fulla deltagande i konflikthantering erkändes som en fråga om internationell fred och säkerhet. Resolutionen var ett resultat av över 20-års lobbying och påverkansarbete som till slut gav resultat.

Den historiska resolutionen ledde en rad svenska kvinno- och fredsorganisationer att samlas år 2003 för att diskutera hur de kunde samarbeta för att resolutionen skulle implementeras och bli verklighet. År 2006 bildades som följd paraplyorganisationen Operation 1325.

Sedan dess har Operation 1325 verkat nationellt och internationellt för att påverka makthavare och civilsamhället att ta säkerhetsrådsresolution 1325 i större beaktning. Kvinnors perspektiv på säkerhet ska genomsyra allt svenskt fredsbyggande arbete, inte minst diplomatiska relationer, utvecklingssamarbete, och militära och civila insatser.

Genom information och utbildning, i Sverige och internationellt, arbetar organisationen för att öka kvinnors inflytande i fredsprocesser och i konfliktlösning. Operation 1325 förordar, informerar, utbildar och skapar plattformar för debatt och dialog för att påverka beslutsfattare, det civila samhället och allmänheten med syftet att implementera FN:s säkerhetsråds resolution 1325 om kvinnor, fred och säkerhet. Trots många framsteg har gjorts sedan FN:s säkerhetsrådsresolution 1325 antogs år 2000, utesluts kvinnor alltjämt från processer som fredssamtal och förhandlingar. Operation 1325 arbetar därför med att utbilda kvinnliga medlare, bygger nätverk för aktiva medlare och stärker kvinnors deltagande i fred och säkerhetsfrågor.

Exempelvis genomförde vi tillsammans med Palestinian Centre for Peace and Democracy (PCPD) "Women's Mediation School" i Palestina för medling och nätverkande. Projektet syftade till att öka makt och aktörskap hos unga kvinnor under 30 år, genom att stödja lokala kvinnliga ledare, aktivister och kvinnoorganisationer. Detta för att stärka unga kvinnors ledarskap och politiska deltagande i det civila samhället, och därigenom främja konfliktlösning och fredsbyggande. Kvinnorna deltog i aktiviteter som anordnades av PCPD och andra palestinska civilsamhällesorganisationer i området.

Rådgivare i Multilaterala Forum

Operation 1325 spelar en viktig roll som rådgivare till flera multilaterala nätverk. Bland annat har vi suttit med i NATO:s civilsamhälles rådgivningspanel för kvinnor, fred och säkerhet – NATO Civil Society Advisory Panel on Women, Peace and Security. Gruppens syfte är att fungera som ett forum för dialog och feedback från civilsamhället till NATO inom frågor som har att göra med kvinnor, fred och säkerhet.

Ett annat exempel är från Commission on the Status of Women vid FN. Operation 1325 bjöds in till en paneldiskussion av vår samarbetsorganisation Global Network of Women Peacebuilders (GNWP). Operation 1325 deltog i panelen tillsammans med representanter från Sverige, Bangladesh och Mali för att diskutera kvinnors sociala skydd, utbildning och arbete.

Utbildningnar i jämställt Fredsbyggande

Operation 1325 har sedan 2003 arbetat med utbildningar och workshops som medel för att stärka kvinnors inflytande i fredsprocesser. Utbildningarna riktar sig bland annat till organisationer i det civila samhället runt om i världen, personal i fredsbevarande insatser och andra aktörer som verkar i konflikt- och postkonfliktområden.

Utbildningarna är i samtliga fall skräddarsydda och bottnar i de behov som uppdragsgivaren ser i sin verksamhet.

I Palestina lever kvinnor i ett samhälle präglat av patriarkala strukturer och normer som placerar kvinnor utanför den offentliga sfären och inom den privata. Vår verksamhet i Palestina förser kvinnor med verktyg för att både förändra och stärka kvinnors rättigheter och deltagande i beslutsfattande och fredsbyggande processer.

Operation 1325 har arbetat med kvinnoorganisationer i Palestina sedan starten av vår verksamehet. Fokuset i projekten ligger på att öka kunskapen om kvinnors rättigheter och kvinnors roll i fredsförmedling, samt att stärka kvinnor att delta i fredsprocesser.

De senaste åren har vi haft många projekt och samarbeten i Palestina. Under 2023 startades det kommunikationsprojektet Operation 1325:s MENA program med syftet att öka kvinnors deltagande i fredsprocesser.

De senaste åren har vi haft mycket samarbete med våra partners Palestinian Center for Peace and Democracy (PCPD) och Palestinian Working Women Society (PWWSD).

Samarbete med våra partners i Palestina sträcker sig tillbaka många år. Tidigare och nuvarande projekt har gett oss möjlighet och utrymme för kontinuerlig kommunikation och samråd.

Liknande projekt har genomförts i bl a Jemen.

Slutkommentar

För att kvinnor ska känna sig mer trygga är det av yttersta vikt att de är medvetna om sina mänskliga rättigheter, att de organiserar sig lokalt, nationellt och internationellt, lär sig hur de kan påverka allmänheten, beslutsfattare osv. I denna artikel har jag nämnt hur den svenska organisationen Operation 1325 arbetar med några av sina projekt. Beroede på den politiska situationen i flera landet samt svårigheten i Sverige att få medel arbetar vi bara i Palestina för närvarande. Vi fortsätter dock att hålla kontakt med våra partners i Sudan, Turkiet och andra länder och hoppas att vi ska kunna återuppta vårt arbete där i framtiden.

What Makes Me Feel Safe

Valentina Uspenskaya, Russia, university lecturer, 2024

What makes me feel safe?

There was your question.

Being safe and feeling safe.

(A few days ago, I was worried about being at ease because of the high fever; I have been in danger of ending up in the hospital – so I feel safe now).

What makes me feel safe?

Now what is happening or will happen around me?

The feeling of home: peace, quiet, classical music to reading/re-reading good old books; and my good old friend by my side.

I just mentioned the word "peace" as a sign of peace in the home, but immediately realize what a great meaning that word has for me – a citizen of the world – especially today. What's more – irony of fate – by writing a book "From a Culture of War to a Culture of Peace" ...

And then the sense of security disappears, slips away, and I feel anxious for all of us. Only WITHOUT danger, surely, can there be a sense of security?

When I look at this photo, I feel really safe

(homemade candle holder made by my granddaughter Alice as a New Year present to me)